Oracle Certification Prep

Study Guide for

1Z0-047: Oracle Database SQL Expert

Matthew Morris

Study Guide for Oracle Database SQL Expert (Exam 1Z0-047) Rev 1.1

ISBN-13: 978-1475152432
ISBN-10: 1475152434

Table of Contents

What to Expect from the Test..10

What to Expect from this Study Guide 11

Additional Study Resources 12

Retrieving Data Using the SQL SELECT Statement 13

    List the capabilities of SQL SELECT statements............................13

        Pseudocolumns..13

        Expressions 14

        Arithmetic Operators & Precedence....................................15

        SQL Functions..17

    Execute a basic SELECT statement...17

    Describe how schema objects work 18

Restricting and Sorting Data 19

    Limit the rows that are retrieved by a query 19

        DISTINCT | UNIQUE..19

        WHERE Clause..20

    Sort the rows that are retrieved by a query 20

Using Single-Row Functions to Customize Output............................23

    Describe various types of functions that are available in SQL 23

        Numeric Functions 23

        Character Functions 24

        Datetime Functions..25

    Use character, number, and date functions in SELECT statements 26

    Describe the use of conversion functions 29

Reporting Aggregated Data Using the Group Functions 30

Identify the available group functions 30

Describe the use of group functions 31

Group data by using the GROUP BY clause 32

Include or exclude grouped rows by using the HAVING clause 33

Displaying Data from Multiple Tables..35

Write SELECT statements to access data from more than one table using equijoins and nonequijoins 37

Join a table to itself by using a self-join 40

View data that generally does not meet a join condition by using outer joins...40

Generate a Cartesian product of all rows from two or more tables......43

Using Subqueries to Solve Queries 45

Define subqueries 46

Describe the types of problems that subqueries can solve 46

List the types of subqueries 49

Write single-row and multiple-row subqueries 49

Using the Set Operators...52

Describe set operators...52

Use a set operator to combine multiple single queries 53

Control the order of rows returned 55

Manipulating Data 58

Describe each data manipulation language (DML) statement 58

Insert rows into a table 59

Update rows in a table...59

Delete rows from a table 59

Control transactions 60

Using DDL Statements to Create and Manage Tables 61

Categorize the main database objects.................................61

Review the table structure 62

List the data types that are available for columns..................63

Create a simple table 64

Explain how constraints are created at the time of table creation 66

Creating Other Schema Objects..69

Create simple and complex views.......................................69

Retrieve data from views...71

Create, maintain, and use sequences 72

Create and maintain indexes 74

Create private and public synonyms....................................76

Managing Objects with Data Dictionary Views.........................80

Use the data dictionary views to research data on your objects..........80

Query various data dictionary views....................................82

Controlling User Access 84

Differentiate system privileges from object privileges 84

Grant privileges on tables 86

View privileges in the data dictionary.................................87

Grant roles 89

Distinguish between privileges and roles 89

Managing Schema Objects...91

Add constraints 91

Create indexes 94

Create indexes using the CREATE TABLE statement 96

Creating function-based indexes 97

Drop columns and set column UNUSED 97

Perform FLASHBACK operations 99

Create and use external tables 104

Manipulating Large Data Sets 106

Manipulate data using subqueries.....................................106

Describe the features of multitable INSERTs 108

Use the following types of multitable INSERTs (Unconditional,
Conditional and Pivot) 108

Merge rows in a table 114

Track the changes to data over a period of time 115

Generating Reports by Grouping Related Data 117

Use the ROLLUP operation to produce subtotal values.......117

Use the CUBE operation to produce crosstabulation values 118

Use the GROUPING function to identify the row values created by
ROLLUP or CUBE 119

Use GROUPING SETS to produce a single result set 120

Managing Data in Different Time Zones 122

Use Various datetime functions..122

Retrieving Data Using Subqueries...129

Write a multiple-column subquery 129

Use scalar subqueries in SQL 131

Solve problems with correlated subqueries 132

Update and delete rows using correlated subqueries..........132

Use the EXISTS and NOT EXISTS operators 133

Use the WITH clause 134

Hierarchical Retrieval...136

Interpret the concept of a hierarchical query.....................136

Create a tree-structured report 137

Format hierarchical data 139

Exclude branches from the tree structure 141

Regular Expression Support 143

Using Meta Characters 143

Regular Expression Functions 144

Replacing Patterns 145

Regular Expressions and Check Constraints 146

What to Expect from the Test

The test consists of 70 multiple choice or multiple answer questions. The passing score listed on Oracle Education at this time is 66%, but as with all Oracle certification tests, they note it is subject to change. This test contains a much higher number of exhibits than the average for Oracle certification exams.

As you would expect a significant percentage of the questions will involve recognizing what the result of one or more SQL statements will be. In some cases you'll be given a single SQL statement and asked what will happen when it runs. In others, you'll be given a desired result and be asked which of the answers will produce that result. To do well on the test you have to be fairly good at running SQL in your head. If you're contemplating taking this test, you should be well aware that writing SQL that doesn't produce an error when executed is fairly easy. Writing SQL that produces the <u>desired</u> data is a good bit more difficult. You'll also need to recognize common SQL functions, understand what the results of DDL operations are, and be able to differentiate between legal and illegal syntax. This is a test that comes fairly close to testing what it should. You really have to understand SQL to do well on the exam. You'll also need to be able to read and understand entity relationship diagrams, as the vast majority of the exhibits will feature one.

Many of the ERDs are fairly complex and only a tiny portion is really crucial to answering the question. For me, in better than half the cases, viewing the ERD was not required in order to answer the question. Reading the question before viewing the exhibit is likely to save you a good bit of time in the test. In some cases, you'll be able to skip the exhibit entirely, and when you need to view it, you'll know what to be looking for. Also, when dealing with questions where the answer is one or more SQL statements, look though <u>all</u> of the answers. Generally at least one will have an obvious flaw that rules it out as a correct answer. Ruling out one or two of the possibilities will allow you to concentrate on the remaining answers.

What to Expect from this Study Guide

This document is built around the subject matter topics that Oracle Education has indicated will be tested. I've gathered together material from several Oracle documentation sources along with results from numerous SQL queries similar to what you'll see on the test. The guide has a significant percentage of the information and operations that you must be familiar with in order to pass the test.

This guide isn't intended to teach you how to write SQL statements. As a general rule, this exam should not be your first Oracle Certification. Most people who are planning to take this exam, will already have completed **1Z0-051 Oracle Database 11g: SQL Fundamentals I** or an equivalent test. The guidelines for 1Z0-051 have a lot of areas in common with 1Z0-047, albeit at a lower level of complexity.

What this guide is intended to do is to present the information that will be covered on the exam at the level it will likely be asked. The guide assumes that you already are an experienced SQL developer and therefore does not start from ground zero on each topic. The result is intended to be a much shorter read that contains the meat of the information you'll need to know without being surrounded by a lot of fluff that you won't. If you really need to have the data at a lower level then this Guide may not be for you – or at least should be used in conjunction with a second resource. I highly recommend on all certification tests that you utilize two or three resources for your study plan.

Additional Study Resources

The companion website to this series is www.oraclecertificationprep.com. The site contains many additional resources that can be used to study for this exam (and others). From the entry page of the website, click on the 'Exams' button, and then select the link for this test. The Exam Details page contains links to the following information sources:

- Applicable Oracle documentation.
- Third-party books relevant to the exam.
- White papers and articles on Oracle Learning Library on topics covered in the exam.
- Articles on the Web that may be useful for the exam.

The website will <u>never</u> link to unauthorized content such as brain dumps or illegal content such as copyrighted material made available without the consent of the author. I cannot guarantee the accuracy of the content links. While I have located the data and scanned it to ensure that it is relevant to the given exam, I did not write it and have not proofread it from a technical standpoint. The material on the Oracle Learning Library is almost certain to be completely accurate and most of the other links come from highly popular Oracle support websites and are created by experienced Oracle professionals.

I recommend that you use more than one source of study materials whenever you are preparing for a certification. Reading information presented from multiple different viewpoints can help to give you a more complete picture of any given topic. The links on the website can help you to do this. Fully understanding the information covered in this certification is not just valuable so that getting a passing score is more likely – it will also help you in your career. I guarantee that in the long run, any knowledge you gain while studying for this certification will provide more benefit to you than any piece of paper or line on your resume.

Retrieving Data Using the SQL SELECT Statement

A query is a database operation that retrieves rows from one or more tables or views. In this context, a top-level SELECT statement is called a query. If there is a second SELECT nested within the first, it is called a subquery.

List the capabilities of SQL SELECT statements

SELECT statements are used to retrieve information from database tables. When a SELECT statement retrieves data, it can do the following three types of work:

- **Selection** -- You can filter the SELECT statement to choose only the rows that you want to be returned.
- **Projection** -- You can choose only the columns that you want to be returned by your query.
- **Joining** -- You can use the SQL JOIN operators to link two or more tables to allow you to return data that is stored in more than one table.

In addition to retrieving and manipulating data that exists in database tables, a SELECT statement can return results that are not stored in tables. There are several ways this can be done. The use of pseudocolumns, expressions, and SQL functions are some of the most common.

Pseudocolumns

A pseudocolumn in Oracle in many ways behaves like a regular table column, but is not actually stored in the database. They can be referenced by SELECT statements, but they cannot be inserted, updated or deleted. Pseudocolumns are similar to a function without arguments in how they act. The two pseudocolumns that exist for all SQL statements are listed below. There are others which will be referenced later that exist for specific operations.

- **ROWNUM** -- For each row returned by a query, this pseudocolumn returns a number indicating the order in which Oracle returns the row.
- **ROWID** -- For each row in the database, this pseudocolumn returns the address of the row.

Expressions

Expressions in the select list of a SQL statement include essentially everything except a bare column name. They could be literals, column data that has been modified by operators, or SQL functions.

- **Text Literals** -- Use to specify values whenever 'string' appears in the syntax of expressions, conditions, SQL functions, and SQL statements. Text literals are always surrounded by single quotation marks.

```
SELECT 'Fred' AS STRING_LIT
FROM dual;
STRING_LIT
----------
Fred
```

- **Numeric Literals** -- Use numeric literal notation to specify fixed and floating-point numbers.

```
SELECT 14.5 AS NUM_LIT
FROM dual;

NUM_LIT
-------
14.5
```

- **Datetime Literals** -- You can specify a date value as a string literal, or you can convert a character or numeric value to a date value using the TO_DATE function.

```
SELECT '10-JAN-12' AS STRING_LIT,
       TO_DATE('01/10/2012', 'MM/DD/YYYY') AS TD_LIT
FROM dual;

STRING_LIT TD_LIT
---------- ---------
10-JAN-12  10-JAN-12
```

- **Interval Literals** -- Interval literals specify a period of time. The interval can be expressed in terms of years and months, or in terms of days, hours, minutes, and seconds. The two supported interval literals are YEAR TO MONTH and DAY TO SECOND.

```
SELECT INTERVAL '12-2' YEAR TO MONTH AS 'MONTHS-DAYS'
FROM dual;

MONTHS-DAYS
-----------
12-2


SELECT INTERVAL '10:22' MINUTE TO SECOND AS 'DY
HR:MIN:SEC.FRAC_SEC'
FROM dual;

DY HR:MIN:SEC.FRAC_SEC
----------------------
0 0:10:22.0
```

Arithmetic Operators & Precedence

Arithmetic operators can be used with one or two arguments to add, subtract, multiply, and divide numeric values. Some operators can also be used in datetime and interval arithmetic. The arguments used must resolve to numeric data types or to a data type that can be implicitly converted to a numeric type.

```
SELECT 4+4
FROM dual;

4+4
---
  8


SELECT SYSDATE, SYSDATE+4
FROM dual;

SYSDATE    SYSDATE+4
---------  ---------
27-MAR-12 31-MAR-12
```

Precedence is the order in which different operators in the same expression are evaluated. Oracle evaluates operators with higher precedence before evaluating those with lower precedence. If there are operators with equal precedence, they are evaluated from left to right within the expression. The plus and minus signs can be used in either a unary fashion or a binary fashion depending on whether they are applied to one or two operands. For example, '-1' is a unary operator and evaluates to 'negative one'. By contrast, '4 - 1' is a binary operator and evaluates to 'four minus one'. The arithmetic operators and their precedence follow:

1. **+, - (as unary operators)** -- Identity, negation,
2. ***, /** -- Multiplication, division
3. **+, - (as binary operators)** -- Addition, subtraction

```
SELECT 3 + 2 * 4
FROM dual;

3+2*4
-----
   11
```

Parentheses can be used to change the order in which the operators are evaluated. When parentheses are nested, the most deeply nested operators are evaluated first:

```
SELECT (3 + 2) * 4
FROM dual;

(3+2)*4
-------
     20
```

When a negative is used as a unary operator, it takes precedence over multiplication or division:

```
SELECT -2 * 6
FROM dual;

-2*6
----
 -12
```

SQL Functions

The use of SQL functions can also generate results that are not stored in database tables. SQL functions will be discussed in more depth in a later section.

Execute a basic SELECT statement

The most basic SELECT statement consists of the SELECT keyword, a list of one or more columns (referred to as the select_list), the FROM keyword, and a table or view (referred to as the table_reference).

```
SELECT apt_id, apt_name, apt_abbr
FROM   airports;

APT_ID APT_NAME                         APT_ABBR
------ ------------------------------- --------
     1 Orlando, FL                      MCO
     2 Atlanta, GA                      ATL
     3 Miami, FL                        MIA
     4 Jacksonville, FL                 JAX
     5 Dallas/Fort Worth                DFW
```

You can use the asterisk wildcard to select the complete set of columns (excluding pseudocolumns) from all tables listed in the FROM clause. You can prefix the asterisk with a table name or table alias to return all columns from a single table if the statement contains a JOIN. When the asterisk is used in a SELECT, the columns will be returned in the order indicated by the COLUMN_ID column of the *_TAB_COLUMNS data dictionary view for the table reference. Any columns that have been marked as UNUSED by the ALTER TABLE SET UNUSED statement will not be returned.

```
SELECT *
FROM   airports;

APT_ID APT_NAME                         APT_ABBR
------ ------------------------------- --------
     1 Orlando, FL                      MCO
     2 Atlanta, GA                      ATL
     3 Miami, FL                        MIA
     4 Jacksonville, FL                 JAX
     5 Dallas/Fort Worth                DFW
```

Describe how schema objects work

Objects in the Oracle Database fall into two broad classes: schema objects and non-schema objects. If an object is associated with a particular schema, then it is a schema object. Conversely, if not, it is a non-schema object. A database schema is owned by and has the same name as an Oracle database user. The schema itself is defined as a collection of logical structures of data, or objects. Schema objects are created and manipulated via SQL statements. A partial list of schema objects follows:

- Constraints
- Database triggers
- Indexes
- Sequences
- Synonyms
- Tables
- Views

Nonschema Objects are also stored in the database and can be created and manipulated with SQL. However, they are not contained in a schema and (with the exception of users) have no affinity to any particular schema. A partial list of these includes:

- Directories
- Roles
- Rollback segments
- Tablespaces
- Users

Restricting and Sorting Data

The ability to retrieve specific information from a database is possibly the most important capability of SQL. Limiting the rows being returned and defining the order they should be returned in are both significant parts of that functionality.

Limit the rows that are retrieved by a query

DISTINCT | UNIQUE

One of the ways in which to limit the amount of data returned by a query it to display only one result when the table(s) being queried have multiple copies of duplicate data. This can be done using either the DISTINCT or UNIQUE keywords. When a row contains matching values for **every** expression in the select list, the DISTINCT/UNIQUE keyword will only return a single row. It is not possible to use DISTINCT/UNIQUE if one or more of the expressions being returned is a LOB column. The two statements below show the effect of adding the DISTINCT keyword to a query.

```
SELECT act_body_style, act_decks
FROM   aircraft_types;

ACT_BODY_STYLE ACT_DECKS
-------------- ----------
Wide           Double
Wide           Single
Narrow         Single
Narrow         Single


SELECT DISTINCT act_body_style, act_decks
FROM   aircraft_types;

ACT_BODY_STYLE ACT_DECKS
-------------- ----------
Wide           Single
Wide           Double
Narrow         Single
```

WHERE Clause

The WHERE clause of SQL statements allows you to create conditions that rows must meet in order to be returned by the query. The conditions in the clause may be extremely simple or mind-numbingly complex. If you omit the WHERE clause, all rows of the table or tables in the query will be returned by the SQL (although the use of DISTINCT/UNIQUE would cause only the unique results to be displayed). If columns are aliased in the SELECT clause, the aliases cannot be used in the WHERE clause.

```
SELECT  *
FROM    aircraft_types
WHERE   act_decks = 'Single';

ACT_ID ACT_NAME       ACT_BODY_STYLE ACT_DECKS  ACT_SEATS
------ -------------- -------------- ---------- ---------
     2 Boeing 767     Wide           Single           350
     3 Boeing 737     Narrow         Single           200
     4 Boeing 757     Narrow         Single           240
```

Sort the rows that are retrieved by a query

The ORDER BY clause of a SQL query allows you to order the rows selected by a query. It's possible to sort by a single column or by multiple columns (or expressions). When sorting by multiple columns, the precedence of the sort order will be determined by the position of the expression in the ORDER BY clause. The leftmost expression will provide the initial sort order and each expression to the right will be evaluated in turn. By default, data is sorted in ascending order (1-2-3-4 / a-b-c-d). One item of note is the fact that upper and lower case characters don't sort together. When Oracle sorts by character values, it is actually using the ASCII values for the logic. Because of this, a lower case 'a' will sort *higher* than an upper case 'Z'. In addition, numeric data in a character field does not sort as you would expect. For example, if you were to sort table rows with values containing '1', '2', and '100' in ascending order, the result would be 1-100-2. To sort number data in a character field in numeric order, you would have to use the TO_NUMBER function against the column in the ORDER BY clause to convert the data for sort purposes.

NULLS are sorted last when a sort is in ascending order and first when descending. This behavior can be reversed by adding NULLS LAST when sorting in descending order or NULLS FIRST when sorting in ascending order.

It is not possible to use LONG or LOB columns in an ORDER BY clause.

When specifying the expressions to sort by, you can use either the expression itself, or its position in the SELECT list. Using the position rather than the expression can be useful of the expression being sorted on is complex. It is also useful when sorting compound queries using the set operators (UNION, INTERSECT, MINUS) where the column names may not match. Set operators will be discussed in a later section.

```
SELECT *
FROM    airports
ORDER BY apt_name;

APT_ID APT_NAME                          APT_ABBR
------ ----------------------------- --------
     2 Atlanta, GA                       ATL
     5 Dallas/Fort Worth                 DFW
     4 Jacksonville, FL                  JAX
     3 Miami, FL                         MIA
     1 Orlando, FL                       MCO


SELECT *
FROM    airports
ORDER BY 2;

APT_ID APT_NAME                          APT_ABBR
------ ----------------------------- --------
     2 Atlanta, GA                       ATL
     5 Dallas/Fort Worth                 DFW
     4 Jacksonville, FL                  JAX
     3 Miami, FL                         MIA
     1 Orlando, FL                       MCO
```

To reverse the sort order of columns, you can use the descending operator, DESC.

```
SELECT  *
FROM    airports
ORDER BY 2 DESC;

APT_ID APT_NAME                    APT_ABBR
------ ---------------------- --------
     1 Orlando, FL                 MCO
     3 Miami, FL                   MIA
     4 Jacksonville, FL            JAX
     5 Dallas/Fort Worth           DFW
     2 Atlanta, GA                 ATL
```

If a column is sorted on more than one column, the default sort order on all columns is ascending. If you want to change multiple columns to sort in descending order, each would need its own DESC keyword.

Using Single-Row Functions to Customize Output

When a single row functions is included in a SQL query, it will generate one result for each table row returned. Single row functions can be used in the following locations:

- SELECT lists
- WHERE clauses
- START WITH clauses
- CONNECT BY clauses
- HAVING clauses

Describe various types of functions that are available in SQL

SQL functions are built into the Oracle Database and can be used in various SQL statements. SQL functions should not be confused with user-defined functions written in PL/SQL. There are too many SQL functions available in Oracle to discuss all of them in this guide. I'll define some of the more common functions that might appear on the test. For more information, you should investigate the Oracle SQL Language Reference manual.

Numeric Functions

ABS
Syntax: ABS(*n*)
Purpose: ABS returns the absolute value of *n*.

```
SELECT ABS(-5) "Abs_Ex"
FROM dual;

Abs_Ex
----------
5
```

ROUND(number)

Syntax: ROUND(*n, integer*)

Purpose: ROUND returns *n* rounded to *integer* places to the right of the decimal point. If *integer* is not supplied, then *n* is rounded to zero places. If the *integer* value is negative, then *n* is rounded off to the left of the decimal point.

```
SELECT ROUND(127.623, 1)   "Round_Ex1",
       ROUND(127.623)      "Round_Ex2",
       ROUND(127.623, -1)  "Round_Ex3"
FROM dual;

Round_Ex1   Round_Ex2   Round_Ex3
----------  ----------  ----------
127.6       127         120
```

Character Functions

INITCAP

Syntax: INITCAP(*char*)

Purpose: INITCAP returns *char*, with the first letter of each word in uppercase, and all other letters in lowercase. The delimiter used to determine words are white space or non alphanumeric characters.

```
SELECT INITCAP('john jones') "Initcap_Ex"
FROM dual;

Initcap_Ex
---------
John Jones
```

LOWER

Syntax: LOWER (*char*)

Purpose: LOWER returns *char*, with all letters lowercase.

```
SELECT LOWER('John Jones') "Lower_Ex"
FROM DUAL;

Lower_EX
----------------
john jones
```

LPAD
Syntax: LPAD(*expr1, n, expr2*)
Purpose: LPAD returns *expr1*, left-padded to length *n* characters with the sequence of characters in *expr2*. If *expr2* is not specified, then the default value is a single space.

```
SELECT LPAD('Page 1', 14, '.') "Lpad_Ex"
FROM DUAL;

Lpad_Ex
---------------
........Page 1
```

LTRIM
Syntax: TRIM(*char, set*)
Purpose: LTRIM removes from the left end of *char* all of the characters contained in *set*. If *set* is not specified, it defaults to a single space.

```
SELECT LTRIM('\----/DATA\----/', '/\-') "Ltrim_Ex"
FROM DUAL;

Ltrim_Ex
----------
DATA\----/
```

Datetime Functions

ADD_MONTHS
Syntax: ADD_MONTHS(*date, integer*)
Purpose: ADD_MONTHS returns the supplied *date* plus *integer* months.

```
SELECT TO_CHAR(ADD_MONTHS('10-MAR-11', 1), 'DD-MON-YY')
"Add_months_Ex"
FROM dual;

Add_months_Ex
-------------
10-APR-11
```

LAST_DAY
Syntax: LAST_DAY(*date*)
Purpose: Returns the last day of the month that contains *date*.

```
SELECT LAST_DAY('12-MAR-11') "Last_day_Ex"
FROM dual;

Last_day_Ex
-----------
30-MAY-09
```

MONTHS_BETWEEN
Syntax: MONTHS_BETWEEN(*date1, date2*)
Purpose: MONTHS_BETWEEN returns number of months between *date1* and *date2*. If *date1* is later than *date2*, then the result is positive. If *date1* is earlier than *date2*, then the result is negative. If *date1* and *date2* are either the same days of the month or both last days of months, then the result is an integer.

```
SELECT MONTHS_BETWEEN('02-JAN-12', '04-JUN-12')
"Months_Between_Ex"
FROM DUAL;

Months_Between_Ex
-----------------
-5.0645161290322580645161290322580645161613
```

Use character, number, and date functions in SELECT statements

The character functions of Oracle modify or provide information regarding character datatypes in Oracle. Character SQL functions can be used in the SELECT clause in order to modify the data returned by a statement, such as the following that transforms airport names to upper-case:

```
SELECT UPPER(apt_name) APT_NAME, apt_abbr
FROM   airports

APT_NAME                             APT_ABBR
-----------------------------        ---------
ORLANDO, FL                          MCO
ATLANTA, GA                          ATL
MIAMI, FL                            MIA
JACKSONVILLE, FL                     JAX
DALLAS/FORT WORTH                    DFW
```

You can also use SQL functions in the WHERE clause to create custom conditions that will locate specific rows. In the example below, the airport name is upper cased, and then the third character pulled out via the SUBSTR function to return all airports with 'L' or 'l' as the third letter.

```
SELECT apt_name, apt_abbr
FROM   airports
WHERE  SUBSTR(UPPER(apt_name), 3, 1) = 'L'

APT_NAME                             APT_ABBR
-----------------------------        ---------
Orlando, FL                          MCO
Atlanta, GA                          ATL
Dallas/Fort Worth                    DFW
```

Just as character functions alter or provide information about character data, numeric functions perform operations against numeric data. In the following example, the annual salary of employees is divided by the number of hours in a work year, and the result rounded to two decimal places with the ROUND function:

```
SELECT emp_first, emp_last, ROUND(salary / 2080, 2) AS
HOURLY_SAL
FROM   employees
WHERE  emp_job = 'Pilot';

EMP_FIRST       EMP_LAST          HOURLY_SAL
-------------   ----------------  ----------
John            Jones                  46.88
Top             Gun                    43.99
Phil            McCoy                  44.95
James           Thomas                 47.36
John            Picard                 45.43
Luke            Skytalker              43.27
Dell            Aptop                  42.07
Noh             Kia                    44.35
```

Date SQL functions in turn are used to generate information from DATE data types. In the below example, the MONTHS_BETWEEN function is used to determine the number of months it has been since each of the pilots was hired. Note that while two DATE types are passed to the function, a NUMBER type is returned. The value returned by SQL functions is not always the same as the value passed to it.

```
SELECT emp_first, emp_last, MONTHS_BETWEEN(SYSDATE,
start_date) AS months_since_hire
FROM    employees
WHERE   emp_job = 'Pilot';
```

```
EMP_FIRST       EMP_LAST        MONTHS_SINCE_HIRE
-------------   -------------   -----------------
John            Jones           203.57773484169653524492234169
Top             Gun             185.48096064814814814814814814
Phil            McCoy           189.60999290621266427718040621
James           Thomas          154.51321871266427718040621266
John            Picard          124.54547677718040621266427718
Luke            Skytalker       114.57773484169653524492234169
Dell            Aptop           103.19063806750298685782556750
Noh             Kia             92.67450903524492341696535244
```

The MONTH_SINCE_HIRE value is really awkward in the above example. Because the result of the MONTHS_BETWEEN function is a NUMBER type, we can apply the numeric function TRUNC to the result to clean it up:

```
SELECT emp_first, emp_last, TRUNC(MONTHS_BETWEEN(SYSDATE,
start_date)) AS months_since_hire
FROM    employees
WHERE   emp_job = 'Pilot';
```

```
EMP_FIRST       EMP_LAST        MONTHS_SINCE_HIRE
-------------   -------------   -----------------
John            Jones                         203
Top             Gun                           185
Phil            McCoy                         189
James           Thomas                        154
John            Picard                        124
Luke            Skytalker                     114
Dell            Aptop                         103
Noh             Kia                            92
```

Describe the use of conversion functions

Conversion functions are used to explicitly convert a value from one data type to another. Data types in Oracle can be converted either explicitly or implicitly. Implicit conversion is handled by the database. If a SQL function is called with an argument of a data type other than the one expected, Oracle will attempt to convert the argument to the expected type. If the conversion is successful, then Oracle will perform the SQL function (if the conversion is unsuccessful, an error will be generated). Examples of two of the most common SQL conversion functions follow. For a complete list, you should refer to the SQL Language Reference manual.

TO_DATE
Syntax: TO_DATE(char, fmt, 'nlsparam')
Purpose: Converts character data to a value of DATE data type. fmt is a datetime model format matching the char input. If fmt is omitted, char must be in the default date format. The optional 'nlsparam' argument specifies the language of the char input.

```
SELECT TO_DATE('February 23, 2012, 2:23 P.M.', 'Month dd,
YYYY, HH:MI A.M.') AS "To_date_Ex"
FROM DUAL;

To_date_Ex
----------
23-FEB-12
```

TO_NUMBER
Syntax: TO_NUMBER(expr, fmt, 'nlsparam')
Purpose: Converts *expr* to a value of NUMBER data type. The *expr* can be a BINARY_DOUBLE value or a character data type containing a number in the format specified by the optional format model *fmt*. The optional 'nlsparam' argument specifies the language of the char input.

```
SELECT TO_NUMBER('$4235.34','FML9,999.99') "To_number_Ex"
FROM dual;

To_number_Ex
------------
4235.34
```

Reporting Aggregated Data Using the Group Functions

Group functions (also known as aggregate functions) return a single result based on multiple rows, as opposed to single-row functions that return one result for each row processed by a given query. Aggregate functions are useful for analyzing data across multiple rows and for locating standout data (like the highest salary or the average age).

Identify the available group functions

As with the Oracle SQL functions, there are too many available to define them all in this guide. Some of the more common ones follow. For a complete list, you should refer to the SQL Language Reference manual.

AVG
Syntax: AVG(DISTINCT/ALL *expr*)
Purpose: AVG returns average value of *expr*.

```
SELECT AVG(salary) "Average"
FROM    employees;

Average
-------
115814.705882352941176470588235294117647
```

MEDIAN
Syntax: MEDIAN(*expr*)
Purpose: MEDIAN takes a numeric or datetime value and returns the middle value or an interpolated value that would be the middle value once the values are sorted.

```
SELECT emp_job, MEDIAN(salary)
FROM employees
GROUP BY emp_job
ORDER BY MEDIAN(salary) DESC;
```

```
EMP_JOB                            MEDIAN(SALARY)
------------------------------     --------------
CEO                                        197500
CFO                                        157000
SVP                                        147150
VP                                         125650
SrDir                                      111000
Mgr                                        101500
Pilot                                       92875
```

MIN

Syntax: MIN(DISTINCT/ALL *expr*)

Purpose: MIN returns minimum value of *expr*.

```
SELECT MIN(start_date) "Earliest"
FROM   employees;

Earliest
---------
10-APR-92
```

Describe the use of group functions

Aggregate functions are intended to group together multiple rows based on a supplied common factor and return a single result for the entire group rather than one result for each row in the table. These functions can appear in select lists and in ORDER BY and HAVING clauses. Aggregates are commonly used in conjunction with the GROUP BY clause in a SELECT statement. When a query contains a GROUP BY clause, the individual elements of the select list can be aggregate functions, GROUP BY expressions, constants, or expressions involving one of these. The aggregate functions will be applied to each group of rows and a single result row returned for each group. When a query contains aggregate functions but no GROUP BY clause, the aggregate functions in the select list are applied to all the rows in the queried table. In this case, one row would be returned for the entire query.

When the GROUP BY clause is present in a SQL statement, you can also make use of the HAVING clause. You can use the HAVING clause to eliminate specific groups from the output based on the results of the aggregate functions, rather than on the values of individual rows. If a

HAVING clause contains a subquery, the subquery is resolved before evaluating the HAVING clause.

Many aggregate functions that take a single argument will accept the use of the DISTINCT/UNIQUE keyword. These will cause an aggregate function to consider only distinct values of the argument expression. Aggregate functions that will accept DISTINCT/UNIQUE will also accept the ALL keyword. This causes an aggregate function to consider all values, including all duplicates. If you specify no keyword, then the default is ALL. The first example below uses the ALL keyword and the second does not.

```
SELECT COUNT(DISTINCT emp_job) distinct_values,
       COUNT(ALL emp_job) AS all_values
FROM   employees;

DISTINCT_VALUES ALL_VALUES
--------------- ----------
             7         17


SELECT COUNT(DISTINCT emp_job) distinct_values,
       COUNT(emp_job) AS all_values
FROM   employees;

DISTINCT_VALUES ALL_VALUES
--------------- ----------
             7         17
```

NULL values are ignored by all of the aggregate functions except COUNT(*), GROUPING, and GROUPING_ID. The COUNT and REGR_COUNT functions will never return a NULL. Their result will be an integer value 0 or greater. All other aggregate functions will return a NULL value if a data set either has no rows or has only rows with NULL as the aggregate function argument.

Group data by using the GROUP BY clause

You specify the GROUP BY clause when you want Oracle to group selected rows based on the value of expr(s) for each row and return a single row of summary information for each group. Expressions in the GROUP BY clause can contain any columns of the tables in the FROM clause, regardless of whether the columns appear in the select list. The GROUP BY clause groups rows but does not guarantee the order of the result set. You must make use of the ORDER BY clause to order the grouped results.

```
SELECT emp_job, MAX(salary) max_salary
FROM    employees
GROUP BY emp_job
```

```
EMP_JOB                                   MAX_SALARY
------------------------------            ----------
VP                                            127800
SrDir                                         111500
SVP                                           149100
Mgr                                           101500
Pilot                                          98500
CEO                                           197500
CFO                                           157000
```

```
SELECT emp_job, MAX(salary) max_salary
FROM    employees
GROUP BY emp_job
ORDER BY emp_job
```

```
EMP_JOB                                   MAX_SALARY
------------------------------            ----------
CEO                                           197500
CFO                                           157000
Mgr                                           101500
Pilot                                          98500
SVP                                           149100
SrDir                                         111500
VP                                            127800
```

Include or exclude grouped rows by using the HAVING clause

The HAVING clause is used to restrict the groups of returned rows to those groups for which the specified condition is TRUE. If the HAVING clause is omitted, then the database returns summary rows for all groups generated by the query. The GROUP BY and HAVING clauses must be after the WHERE clause and hierarchical query clause (hierarchical queries are discussed later in this guide), but before the ORDER BY clause. If you specify both GROUP BY and HAVING, then they can appear in either order.

```
SELECT emp_job, MAX(salary) max_salary
FROM    employees
GROUP BY emp_job
HAVING MAX(salary) > 111500
ORDER BY emp_job
```

```
EMP_JOB                             MAX_SALARY
----------------------------------- ----------
CEO                                     197500
CFO                                     157000
SVP                                     149100
VP                                      127800
```

Displaying Data from Multiple Tables

Any query that combines rows from two or more tables, views, or materialized views must make use of joins. Oracle will perform a join operation any time multiple tables appear in the FROM clause of the query. If multiple tables exist in the FROM clause, the select list can include any columns from any of the tables. When more than one table has a column name in common, any references to duplicated columns must be qualified in all parts of the query. You qualify a column name by prefixing it with the table name followed by a period, or with the table alias followed by a period.

```
SELECT  apt_name, apt_abbr, act_name, act_seats
FROM    airports apt
        INNER JOIN aircraft_fleet afl
        ON apt.apt_id = afl.apt_id
        INNER JOIN aircraft_types act
        ON act.act_id = afl.act_id

APT_NAME                 APT_ABBR ACT_NAME        ACT_SEATS
------------------------ -------- --------------- ---------
Orlando, FL              MCO      Boeing 767            350
Orlando, FL              MCO      Boeing 767            350
Atlanta, GA              ATL      Boeing 757            240
Atlanta, GA              ATL      Boeing 737            200
Miami, FL                MIA      Boeing 747            416
Miami, FL                MIA      Boeing 747            416
Dallas/Fort Worth        DFW      Boeing 767            350
Dallas/Fort Worth        DFW      Boeing 747            416
```

You should understand the various join definitions.

- **EQUIJOIN** -- A join where the condition contains an equality operator. An equijoin combines rows that have equivalent values for the specified columns.
- **NON-EQUIJOIN** -- A join where the condition does not contain an equality operator – (e.g. the operator might be greater than or less than). A non-equijoin combines rows that have non-equivalent values for the specified columns.

- **SELF-JOIN** -- A join of a table back to itself. The given table will appear twice (or more) in the FROM clause. All incarnations should have table aliases to allow you to qualify column names in the join condition and other parts of the query.
- **INNER JOIN** -- An inner join (sometimes called a simple join) is a join of two or more tables that returns only those rows that satisfy the join condition.
- **FULL OUTER JOIN** -- An outer join returns all rows that satisfy the join condition and also returns all of those rows from the tables for which no rows from the other satisfy the join condition.
- **LEFT OUTER JOIN** – A left join is a subset of the outer join where all of the rows in the table identified on the left-side of the join operator are returned and only the rows that meet the join condition are returned from the table on the right side of the operator.
- **RIGHT OUTER JOIN** – A right join is the opposite of the left join. All of the rows in the table identified on the right-side of the join operator are returned and only the rows that meet the join condition are returned from the table on the left side of the operator.
- **CROSS JOIN** -- A cross join is the result when two tables are included in a query but no join condition is specified. When this is the case, Oracle returns the Cartesian product of the two tables (this is sometimes called a Cartesian Join). The Cartesian product is when every row of one table is joined with every row of the other. Generally considered to be useless, cross joins are most often created by mistake.
- **NATURAL JOIN** – A natural join can only be used when the column names and data types used for the join match in both tables. It will perform an inner-equijoin between the two tables.

Note that the above definitions are not exclusive; a JOIN will generally meet more than one definition at a time (i.e. an equijoin that is also an inner join and a self join). Also, if you are used to the old Oracle syntax of left and right joins that made use of the (+) notation, you'll need to forget it for the test. Oracle has deprecated that syntax in favor of the ANSI style so it will not be represented on the exam.

Write SELECT statements to access data from more than one table using equijoins and nonequijoins

The vast majority of JOIN operations use equijoins. In an equijoin the condition is that column A in table one EQUALS column B in table two. In general when there's a need to join two tables, it will be by column data that is exactly equal. The below query uses three equijoins and connects four tables together to generate the required results.

```
SELECT apt_name, act_name, emp_first, emp_last
FROM   airports apt
       INNER JOIN aircraft_fleet afl
       ON apt.apt_id = afl.apt_id
       INNER JOIN aircraft_types act
       ON act.act_id = afl.act_id
       INNER JOIN employees emp
       ON afl.afl_id = emp.afl_id;
```

APT_NAME	ACT_NAME	EMP_FIRST	EMP_LAST
Orlando, FL	Boeing 767	John	Jones
Orlando, FL	Boeing 767	Top	Gun
Atlanta, GA	Boeing 737	Phil	McCoy
Atlanta, GA	Boeing 757	James	Thomas
Miami, FL	Boeing 747	John	Picard
Miami, FL	Boeing 747	Luke	Skytalker
Dallas/Fort Worth	Boeing 747	Dell	Aptop
Dallas/Fort Worth	Boeing 767	Noh	Kia

Because the joins in the above example all are equijoins where the column names and types match in both tables, the NATURAL JOIN could have been used to generate the same result:

```
SELECT apt_name, act_name, emp_first, emp_last
FROM    airports apt
        NATURAL JOIN aircraft_fleet afl
        NATURAL JOIN aircraft_types act
        NATURAL JOIN employees emp;
```

APT_NAME	ACT_NAME	EMP_FIRST	EMP_LAST
Orlando, FL	Boeing 767	John	Jones
Orlando, FL	Boeing 767	Top	Gun
Atlanta, GA	Boeing 737	Phil	McCoy
Atlanta, GA	Boeing 757	James	Thomas
Miami, FL	Boeing 747	John	Picard
Miami, FL	Boeing 747	Luke	Skytalker
Dallas/Fort Worth	Boeing 747	Dell	Aptop
Dallas/Fort Worth	Boeing 767	Noh	Kia

A third equivalent option for the query is the JOIN...USING syntax:

```
SELECT apt_name, act_name, emp_first, emp_last
FROM    airports apt
        JOIN aircraft_fleet afl USING (apt_id)
        JOIN aircraft_types act USING (act_id)
        JOIN employees emp USING (afl_id);
```

APT_NAME	ACT_NAME	EMP_FIRST	EMP_LAST
Orlando, FL	Boeing 767	John	Jones
Orlando, FL	Boeing 767	Top	Gun
Atlanta, GA	Boeing 737	Phil	McCoy
Atlanta, GA	Boeing 757	James	Thomas
Miami, FL	Boeing 747	John	Picard
Miami, FL	Boeing 747	Luke	Skytalker
Dallas/Fort Worth	Boeing 747	Dell	Aptop
Dallas/Fort Worth	Boeing 767	Noh	Kia

Finally a fourth equivalent option for the query is the JOIN...ON syntax. This is equivalent to 'INNER JOIN...ON'. One thing to watch out for is in confusing JOIN...USING with JOIN...ON. When the USING clause is utilized, only the column name(s) for the JOIN get specified. It is always an EQUIJOIN and the join column names must always be the same in both tables. If the join column(s) are in the SELECT list, they should not be qualified with the table name or alias. When the ON syntax is used, the join condition must specify both columns (qualified if they are the same name) and the operator. If the join columns are in the SELECT list and have the same name, they must be qualified with the table name or alias.

```
SELECT apt_name, act_name, emp_first, emp_last
FROM   airports apt
       JOIN aircraft_fleet afl ON (apt.apt_id = afl.apt_id)
       JOIN aircraft_types act ON (afl.act_id = act.act_id)
       JOIN employees emp ON (afl.afl_id = emp.afl_id);
```

APT_NAME	ACT_NAME	EMP_FIRST	EMP_LAST
Orlando, FL	Boeing 767	John	Jones
Orlando, FL	Boeing 767	Top	Gun
Atlanta, GA	Boeing 737	Phil	McCoy
Atlanta, GA	Boeing 757	James	Thomas
Miami, FL	Boeing 747	John	Picard
Miami, FL	Boeing 747	Luke	Skytalker
Dallas/Fort Worth	Boeing 747	Dell	Aptop
Dallas/Fort Worth	Boeing 767	Noh	Kia

On occasion, however, there is a need to perform a non-equijoin. In a non-equijoin, the condition joining the columns of the two tables uses some condition other than EQUALS. In the below example, the EMPLOYEES table is joined to the SALARY_RANGES table. The join operation uses the BETWEEN operator to find which range each employee's salary falls into in order to determine the salary code.

```
SELECT emp.emp_first, emp.emp_last, salary, slr_code
FROM   employees emp
       INNER JOIN salary_ranges slr
       ON emp.salary BETWEEN slr.slr_lowval
                         AND slr.slr_highval
ORDER BY slr_code DESC;
```

EMP_FIRST	EMP_LAST	SALARY	SLR_CODE
Big	Boss	197500	S09
Adam	Smith	157000	S07
Rob	Stoner	149100	S07
Rick	Jameson	145200	S07
Janet	Jeckson	127800	S06
Bill	Abong	123500	S06
Norm	Storm	101500	S05
Fred	Stoneflint	111500	S05
Alf	Alien	110500	S05
Luke	Skytalker	90000	S04
Dell	Aptop	87500	S04
Phil	McCoy	93500	S04
Noh	Kia	92250	S04
Top	Gun	91500	S04
John	Picard	94500	S04
James	Thomas	98500	S04
John	Jones	97500	S04

Join a table to itself by using a self-join

It's sometimes very useful to join a table back to itself when rows in it reference other rows. In the example below, we join the EMPLOYEES table back to itself by using the EMP_ID and EMP_SUPERVISOR columns. In this fashion we're able to display each employee's manager. Later in this guide, we'll use the CONNECT BY capability to create more complete organization charts.

```
SELECT emp.emp_first, emp.emp_last, mgr.emp_first || ' ' ||
mgr.emp_last AS EMP_MANAGER
FROM    employees emp
        LEFT JOIN employees mgr
        ON emp.emp_supervisor = mgr.emp_id
ORDER BY NVL(mgr.emp_supervisor, 0), emp.emp_last,
emp.emp_first
```

EMP_FIRST	EMP_LAST	EMP_MANAGER
Big	Boss	
Rick	Jameson	Big Boss
Adam	Smith	Big Boss
Rob	Stoner	Big Boss
Bill	Abong	Rick Jameson
Janet	Jeckson	Rob Stoner
Fred	Stoneflint	Bill Abong
Alf	Alien	Janet Jeckson
Norm	Storm	Alf Alien
Dell	Aptop	Norm Storm
Top	Gun	Norm Storm
John	Jones	Norm Storm
Noh	Kia	Norm Storm
Phil	McCoy	Norm Storm
John	Picard	Norm Storm
Luke	Skytalker	Norm Storm
James	Thomas	Norm Storm

View data that generally does not meet a join condition by using outer joins

When you use an INNER join to link two tables where column A of table one equals column B of table two, any rows from both tables that don't meet the specified condition aren't returned by the query. In cases where you would like non-matched rows to be returned, you must use one of the OUTER join syntaxes. There are three varieties of OUTER joins. The behavior of the first two is determined by which side of the join operator a table's column appears on. The definitions below use this example:

Table1.Column_A = Table2.Column_B

- **LEFT OUTER JOIN** – Rows from the Table1 will be returned regardless of whether or not there are rows in Table2 where Column_A = Column_B. The 'OUTER' portion of the syntax is optional (i.e. 'LEFT OUTER JOIN' and 'LEFT JOIN' are equivalent)
- **RIGHT OUTER JOIN** – Rows from the Table2 will be returned regardless of whether or not there are rows in Table1 where Column_A = Column_B. The 'OUTER' portion of the syntax is optional (i.e. 'RIGHT OUTER JOIN' and 'RIGHT JOIN' are equivalent)
- **FULL OUTER JOIN** -- Rows from both tables will be returned regardless of whether or not there are rows where Column_A = Column_B.

For the join examples, we'll create the following tables:

```
CREATE TABLE table_A (
  col1     NUMBER,
  col2     VARCHAR2(1)
);

CREATE TABLE table_B (
  col1     NUMBER,
  col2     VARCHAR2(1)
);
```

Now we'll populate them with the below data:

```
INSERT INTO table_A VALUES (1, 'a');
INSERT INTO table_A VALUES (2, 'b');
INSERT INTO table_A VALUES (3, 'c');

INSERT INTO table_B VALUES (2, 'B');
INSERT INTO table_B VALUES (3, 'C');
INSERT INTO table_B VALUES (4, 'D');
```

An INNER JOIN between these two tables produces the following results:

```
SELECT a.col1, a.col2, b.col2
FROM   table_A a
```

```
    INNER JOIN table_B b
    ON a.col1 = b.col1;

COL1 COL2 COL2
---- ---- ----
   2 b    B
   3 c    C
```

Changing to a LEFT JOIN produces the results below. The row in table_A without a matching value in table_B is now displayed. The LEFT JOIN will return rows without matches from the table represented on the left side of the JOIN operator (in this case a.col1).

```
SELECT a.col1, a.col2, b.col2
FROM   table_A a
       LEFT JOIN table_B b
       ON a.col1 = b.col1;

COL1 COL2 COL2
---- ---- ----
   2 b    B
   3 c    C
   1 a
```

Changing to a RIGHT JOIN produces the results below. Now the row in table_B without a matching value in table_A is now displayed. The RIGHT JOIN will return rows without matches from the table represented on the right side of the JOIN operator (in this case b.col1). We could have gotten the same results by continuing to use the LEFT JOIN but reversing the join condition order (i.e. b.col1 = a.col1).

```
SELECT a.col1, a.col2, b.col2
FROM   table_A a
       RIGHT JOIN table_B b
       ON a.col1 = b.col1;

COL1 COL2 COL2
---- ---- ----
   2 b    B
   3 c    C
            D
```

Changing to a FULL OUTER JOIN will cause all rows in both tables to be returned regardless of whether the join condition evaluates to TRUE.

```
SELECT a.col1, a.col2, b.col2
FROM   table_A a
       FULL OUTER JOIN table_B b
       ON a.col1 = b.col1;

COL1 COL2 COL2
---- ---- ----
   2 b    B
   3 c    C
          D
   1 a
```

Generate a Cartesian product of all rows from two or more tables

A Cartesian product, or CROSS JOIN between two tables is something that is generally created by accident. The result of this operation is that every single row of the first table is joined to every single row of the second. The result if either or both of the tables contain many rows can be enormous (the multiple of the rows in the first table times the rows in the second). A Cartesian join between the AIRPORTS table (5 rows) and the AIRCRAFT_TYPES table (4 rows) creates a result with 20 rows. The example below is sorted by the airport and then the aircraft type to highlight the way the rows in these two tables have been joined.

```
SELECT apt_name, apt_abbr, act_name, act_seats
FROM   airports apt
       CROSS JOIN aircraft_types act
ORDER BY apt_name, act_name;

APT_NAME                 APT_ABBR ACT_NAME      ACT_SEATS
-------------------- -------- ------------  ---------
Atlanta, GA              ATL      Boeing 737          200
Atlanta, GA              ATL      Boeing 747          416
Atlanta, GA              ATL      Boeing 757          240
Atlanta, GA              ATL      Boeing 767          350
Dallas/Fort Worth        DFW      Boeing 737          200
Dallas/Fort Worth        DFW      Boeing 747          416
Dallas/Fort Worth        DFW      Boeing 757          240
Dallas/Fort Worth        DFW      Boeing 767          350
Jacksonville, FL         JAX      Boeing 737          200
Jacksonville, FL         JAX      Boeing 747          416
Jacksonville, FL         JAX      Boeing 757          240
Jacksonville, FL         JAX      Boeing 767          350
```

```
Miami, FL              MIA       Boeing 737         200
Miami, FL              MIA       Boeing 747         416
Miami, FL              MIA       Boeing 757         240
Miami, FL              MIA       Boeing 767         350
Orlando, FL            MCO       Boeing 737         200
Orlando, FL            MCO       Boeing 747         416
Orlando, FL            MCO       Boeing 757         240
Orlando, FL            MCO       Boeing 767         350
```

The below query would generate results identical to the above one. Since no join condition is specified, Oracle has no alternative but to join all rows in both tables. A Cartesian product will also result if a join condition is specified, but invalid (assuming the invalid condition is not one that causes the SQL statement to fail altogether).

```
SELECT apt_name, apt_abbr, act_name, act_seats
FROM   airports apt,
       aircraft_types act
ORDER BY apt_name, act_name;
```

Using Subqueries to Solve Queries

Subqueries are generally used to answer questions that contain multiple parts. For example, to determine which pilots fly the same type of aircraft as James Thomas, you can first use a subquery to determine which aircraft James pilots. The original question can then be answered using the parent SELECT statement.

- **Inline View**: A subquery in the FROM clause of a SELECT statement. It possible to nest any number of subqueries in an inline view.
- **Nested Subquery**: A subquery in the WHERE clause of a SELECT statement. You can nest up to 255 levels of subqueries in a nested subquery.

If columns in a subquery have the same name as columns in the outer query and columns from the outer query are referenced in the subquery, then column references are required. You must prefix all references to the column of the table from the containing statement with the table name or alias. It's good practice to prefix the subquery column references as well, but not a requirement.

```
SELECT emp_first, emp_last, emp_job
FROM    employees emp
WHERE   salary > (SELECT slr_highval
                  FROM    salary_ranges
                  WHERE   slr_code = 'S05')

EMP_FIRST   EMP_LAST    EMP_JOB
----------  ----------  ----------
Big         Boss        CEO
Adam        Smith       CFO
Rick        Jameson     SVP
Rob         Stoner      SVP
Bill        Abong       VP
Janet       Jeckson     VP
```

Define subqueries

A subquery is a query that is nested inside another query. The outer query might be a SELECT, INSERT, UPDATE, or DELETE statement (or another subquery). Subqueries can return a single row or multiple rows; a single column or multiple columns. A subquery can be used in any of the following locations:

- The SELECT list
- The FROM clause
- The WHERE clause
- The HAVING clause

Describe the types of problems that subqueries can solve

Create a Table Equivalent to SELECT From

A subquery can be used in the FROM clause of a query as a table-equivalent. When used in this fashion, they are called inline views. The subquery is used to format the table data in a fashion that makes it possible for the outer SELECT to return the desired results. Inline views often aggregate data from the base table.

```
SELECT emp_job, avg_sal, min_sal || ' - ' ||
       max_sal AS salary_range
FROM   (SELECT emp_job, AVG(salary) AVG_SAL,
               MIN(salary) MIN_SAL, MAX(salary) MAX_SAL
        FROM   employees
        GROUP BY emp_job)
ORDER BY max_sal DESC

EMP_JOB    AVG_SAL SALARY_RANGE
---------- ------- -----------------
CEO         197500 197500 - 197500
CFO         157000 157000 - 157000
SVP         147150 145200 - 149100
VP          125650 123500 - 127800
SrDir       111000 110500 - 111500
Mgr         101500 101500 - 101500
Pilot     93156.25 87500 - 98500
```

Generate a Result Set to Filter by

You might use a subquery to answer questions such as which airports have 747s based at them. You could answer that with a subquery such as the below example.

```
SELECT  apt_name, apt_abbr
FROM    airports apt
WHERE   apt.apt_id IN (SELECT apt_id
                       FROM    aircraft_types act
                               INNER JOIN aircraft_fleet afl
                               ON act.act_id = afl.act_id
                       WHERE   act_name = 'Boeing 747')


APT_NAME                       APT_ABBR
--------------------- --------
Miami, FL                      MIA
Dallas/Fort Worth              DFW
```

Generate Projection Columns

When utilized in the SELECT list of a query, scalar subqueries act like SQL functions to generate new expressions.

```
SELECT  emp_first, emp_last, salary,
        (SELECT AVG(salary)
         FROM    employees
         WHERE   emp_job='Pilot') AVG_SALARY
FROM    employees
WHERE   emp_job = 'Pilot';

EMP_FIRST  EMP_LAST    SALARY AVG_SALARY
---------- ---------- ------ ----------
John       Jones       97500   88968.75
Top        Gun         91500   88968.75
Phil       McCoy      105000   88968.75
James      Thomas      98500   88968.75
John       Picard      49500   88968.75
Luke       Skytalker   90000   88968.75
Dell       Aptop       87500   88968.75
Noh        Kia         92250   88968.75
```

Generate Data for an INSERT, UPDATE, or DELETE

A subquery can be used to generate a set of rows to be inserted into a table. Alternately, a scalar subquery could be utilized as the source expressions for an update statement. Finally, a subquery could be used to identify rows that meet a given criteria and pass the result to a delete statement.

This statement would add a new row into the AIRCRAFT_TYPES table for the Boeing 787, pulling some values from the record for the Boeing 767. It does not supply a primary key value, so if the table does not have a trigger in place to provide that data, the INSERT would fail.

```
INSERT INTO aircraft_types (act_name, act_body_style,
act_decks, act_seats)
SELECT 'Boeing 787', act_body_style, act_decks, 300
FROM   aircraft_types
WHERE  act_name = 'Boeing 767';
```

This statement would move all aircraft based in Orlando to Dallas/Ft Worth:

```
UPDATE aircraft_fleet
SET    apt_id = (SELECT apt_id
                 FROM   airports
                 WHERE  apt_abbr = 'DFW')
WHERE  apt_id = (SELECT apt_id
                 FROM   airports
                 WHERE  apt_abbr = 'MCO');
```

This statement would delete any rows from the AIRCRAFT_TYPES table if there is not currently an aircraft of that type in the fleet.

```
DELETE FROM aircraft_types
WHERE  act_id NOT IN (SELECT act_id
                      FROM   aircraft_fleet);
```

When using a subquery in an INSERT statement insert data into a table, the VALUES clause is not used. A subquery inside a VALUES clause is illegal and will generate an error.

List the types of subqueries

At the highest level, there are three classes of subqueries:

- **Single-row subqueries** – A single-row subquery returns a single result row to the parent SQL. When only a single column is returned, it is a special subclass called a scalar subquery. Scalar subqueries can be used in almost every location where you can use an expression, literal value, or a constant.
- **Multiple-row subqueries** -- A multiple-row subquery returns result sets with more than one row to the surrounding SQL. Often they are used to generate results for a SELECT statement or DML operation.
- **Correlated subqueries** – When a subquery references column data from the parent query, the results become dependent on the parent. The parent data can change with each row returned by the parent query. Therefore, unlike a single or multiple-row subquery that runs once when a SQL statement is executed, a correlated subquery must run once for each row of the parent. The results can be useful, but correlated subqueries can create performance problems depending on the execute time of the subquery and the number of rows evaluated in the parent query.

Write single-row and multiple-row subqueries

Following are some examples of single- and multiple-row subqueries. While either type of subquery may be used in the WHERE and HAVING clauses of the parent query, you must use a valid comparison operator. The two lists below show valid operators for single and multiple row subqueries. It's important to note that while multiple-row operators will work correctly if only a single row is returned by a subquery, the reverse is not true. Single row operators will generate an error if more than one row is returned.

Single Row Operators

=	Equal to
>	Greater than
>=	Greater than or equal to
<	Less than
<=	Less than or equal to
<> or !=	Not equal to

Multiple Row Operators

IN	Equal to any member in a list
NOT IN	Not equal to any member in a list
ANY	TRUE when any values match
ALL	TRUE when all values match
EXISTS	TRUE when the subquery returns any rows
NOT EXISTS	TRUE when the subquery returns no rows

The ANY and ALL operators are used to modify the behavior of single row operators:

- **ANY** -- Compares a value to each value in a list or returned by a query. Must be preceded by =, !=, >, <, <=, >=. Evaluates to FALSE if the query returns no rows.
- **ALL**: -- Compares a value to every value in a list or returned by a query. Must be preceded by =, !=, >, <, <=, >=. Evaluates to TRUE if the query returns no rows.

Single-Row Subquery

```
SELECT  apt_name, apt_abbr, act_name, act_seats
FROM    airports apt
        INNER JOIN aircraft_fleet afl
        ON apt.apt_id = afl.apt_id
        INNER JOIN aircraft_types act
        ON act.act_id = afl.act_id
WHERE   afl_id = (SELECT afl_id
                  FROM    employees
                  WHERE   emp_last = 'Picard')


APT_NAME                 APT_ABBR ACT_NAME      ACT_SEATS
---------------------    -------- ------------  ---------
Miami, FL                MIA      Boeing 747          416
```

Multiple-Row Subquery

```
SELECT  apt_name, apt_abbr, act_name, act_seats
FROM    airports apt
        INNER JOIN aircraft_fleet afl
        ON apt.apt_id = afl.apt_id
        INNER JOIN aircraft_types act
        ON act.act_id = afl.act_id
WHERE   afl_id IN (SELECT afl_id
                   FROM    employees
                   WHERE   emp_last IN ('Picard', 'McCoy',
'Aptop')
                   )
```

```
APT_NAME                 APT_ABBR ACT_NAME     ACT_SEATS
---------------------    -------- ------------ ---------
Atlanta, GA              ATL      Boeing 737         200
Miami, FL                MIA      Boeing 747         416
Dallas/Fort Worth        DFW      Boeing 747         416
```

The above query could also resolve the subquery using the = operator modified by the ANY operator:

```
SELECT  apt_name, apt_abbr, act_name, act_seats
FROM    airports apt
        INNER JOIN aircraft_fleet afl
        ON apt.apt_id = afl.apt_id
        INNER JOIN aircraft_types act
        ON act.act_id = afl.act_id
WHERE   afl_id = ANY (SELECT afl_id
                      FROM    employees
                      WHERE   emp_last IN ('Picard', 'McCoy',
                                           'Aptop')
                      )
```

```
APT_NAME                 APT_ABBR ACT_NAME     ACT_SEATS
---------------------    -------- ------------ ---------
Atlanta, GA              ATL      Boeing 737         200
Miami, FL                MIA      Boeing 747         416
Dallas/Fort Worth        DFW      Boeing 747         416
```

Using the Set Operators

Set operators allow you to combine the results from two or more SELECT statements. The results of individual SELECT statements are treated as sets, and SQL set operations are applied against the sets to generate the desired result. Queries joined by set operators are also known as compound queries.

Describe set operators

Oracle supports the following set operations:

- **UNION** – Combines the results of two SELECT operations into a single set. Duplicate rows are removed from the end result.
- **UNION ALL** -- Combines the results of two SELECT operations into a single set. Duplicate rows are included in the end result.
- **INTERSECT** – Returns distinct rows where all selected values exist in both queries.
- **MINUS** – Returns distinct rows selected by the first query but not the second.

All set operators have equal precedence. Any time a SQL statement contains multiple set operators, Oracle will evaluate them from top to bottom unless parentheses are used to explicitly specify a different order. The select lists of every query being combined with SET operators must have the same number of columns and each column position must be in the same data type group. For example, column one in the first SELECT could be a VARCHAR2 field and column one in the second SELECT a CHAR field. However, if column one in the first query is a VARCHAR2 field and column one in the second query is a NUMBER field, Oracle will generate an error.

Columns names returned by the query are determined by the first SELECT statement. An ORDER BY clause can only be placed at the very end of a compound query involving set operators.

Restrictions on the Set Operators
- Set operations cannot be performed on BLOB, CLOB, BFILE, VARRAY, or nested table columns.
- UNION, INTERSECT, and MINUS operators are not valid on LONG columns.
- Expressions in the SELECT list must have an alias in order to be used in the order_by clause.
- Set operators cannot be used with the for_update_clause.
- Set operations are not allowed on SELECT statements containing TABLE collection expressions.

Use a set operator to combine multiple single queries

Following are examples of each of the four types of SET operations. For the examples, we'll use the following tables and data:

```
CREATE TABLE table_setA (
  col1    VARCHAR2(1)
);

CREATE TABLE table_setB (
  col1    VARCHAR2(1)
);

INSERT INTO table_setA VALUES ('A');
INSERT INTO table_setA VALUES ('A');
INSERT INTO table_setA VALUES ('A');
INSERT INTO table_setA VALUES ('A');
INSERT INTO table_setA VALUES ('B');
INSERT INTO table_setA VALUES ('C');

INSERT INTO table_setB VALUES ('B');
INSERT INTO table_setB VALUES ('B');
INSERT INTO table_setB VALUES ('C');
INSERT INTO table_setB VALUES ('C');
INSERT INTO table_setB VALUES ('D');
INSERT INTO table_setB VALUES ('D');
INSERT INTO table_setB VALUES ('D');
```

If the UNION set operator is used to combine results from these two tables, it will produce the distinct values returned by the two queries:

```
SELECT  col1
FROM    table_setA
UNION
SELECT  col1
FROM    table_setB

COL1
----
A
B
C
D
```

If the UNION ALL set operator is used to combine results from these two tables, it will produce all values returned by the two queries. The UNION ALL is the only set operator that does not produce distinct results.

```
SELECT  col1
FROM    table_setA
UNION ALL
SELECT  col1
FROM    table_setB;

COL1
----
A
A
A
A
B
C
B
B
C
C
D
D
D
```

If the INTERSECT set operator is used to combine results from these two tables, it will produce only values returned by both queries.

```
SELECT  col1
FROM    table_setA
INTERSECT
SELECT  col1
FROM    table_setB;

COL1
----
B
C
```

If the MINUS set operator is used to combine results from these two tables, it will produce only values returned by the first query, but not the second. MINUS is the only set operator where the order of the queries will change the results.

```
SELECT  col1
FROM    table_setA
MINUS
SELECT  col1
FROM    table_setB;

COL1
----
A

SELECT  col1
FROM    table_setB
MINUS
SELECT  col1
FROM    table_setA;

COL1
----
D
```

Control the order of rows returned

By default, the output of compound queries is not sorted at all. The output of the individual sets will be returned in groups, and the sorting within the groups is largely indeterminate. It is not allowable to make use of ORDER BY clauses in the individual queries. To sort the results of a compound query, you must place an ORDER BY clause at the end of the statement. This will sort the entire output of the compound query. With compound queries, making use of column position to sort by is often useful. The individual column names of the components may be different. If you use column names or aliases, you must use them from the first SELECT list in the compound query.

The following example orders rows returned from the EMPLOYEES table by the employee's last name, then by their first name. The columns are specified by name.

```
SELECT emp_last, emp_first, salary, start_date
FROM    employees
WHERE   emp_job = 'Pilot'
UNION
SELECT emp_last, emp_first, salary, start_date
FROM    employees
WHERE   emp_job = 'VP'
ORDER BY emp_last, emp_first
```

EMP_LAST	EMP_FIRST	SALARY	START_DATE
Abong	Bill	123500	17-MAY-92
Aptop	Dell	87500	22-AUG-03
Gun	Top	91500	13-OCT-96
Jeckson	Janet	127800	15-APR-02
Jones	John	97500	10-APR-95
Kia	Noh	92250	07-JUL-04
McCoy	Phil	105000	09-JUN-96
Picard	John	49500	11-NOV-01
Skytalker	Luke	90000	10-SEP-02
Thomas	James	98500	12-MAY-99

The following example orders rows returned from the EMPLOYEES table by the start date. The column is specified by position.

```
SELECT emp_last, emp_first, salary, start_date
FROM    employees
WHERE   emp_job = 'Pilot'
UNION
SELECT emp_last, emp_first, salary, start_date
FROM    employees
WHERE   emp_job = 'VP'
ORDER BY 4
```

```
EMP_LAST    EMP_FIRST    SALARY  START_DATE
----------  ----------   ------  ----------
Abong       Bill         123500  17-MAY-92
Jones       John          97500  10-APR-95
McCoy       Phil         105000  09-JUN-96
Gun         Top           91500  13-OCT-96
Thomas      James         98500  12-MAY-99
Picard      John          49500  11-NOV-01
Jeckson     Janet        127800  15-APR-02
Skytalker   Luke          90000  10-SEP-02
Aptop       Dell          87500  22-AUG-03
Kia         Noh           92250  07-JUL-04
```

Manipulating Data

Data Manipulation Language (DML) is the name given to the SQL statements used to manage data in the Oracle database. DML statements include INSERT, UPDATE, DELETE and MERGE. The SELECT statement could technically be considered a DML statement but is seldom considered one in practice.

Describe each data manipulation language (DML) statement

Data manipulation language statements are utilized to manage data in existing schema objects. DML statements do not modify information in the data dictionary and do not implicitly commit the current transaction. The most commonly identified DML commands are:

- **INSERT** – Used to populate data in tables. It is possible to insert one row into one table, one row into multiple tables, multiple rows into one table, or multiple rows into multiple tables.
- **UPDATE** – Used to alter data that already been inserted into a database table. An UPDATE can affect a single row or multiple rows, a single column or multiple columns. The WHERE clause will determine which rows in the table are altered. A single UPDATE statement can only act on a single table.
- **DELETE** – Used to remove previously inserted rows from a table. The command can remove a single row or multiple rows from a table. When executed with no WHERE clause, it will remove all rows from the target table. It is not possible to delete only certain columns – the entire row is deleted or it is not. A single DELETE statement can only act on a single table.
- **MERGE** – Used for hybrid DML operations. The MERGE can insert, update and delete rows in a table all in a single statement. There is no operation that a MERGE can perform that could not be performed by a combination of INSERT, UPDATE and DELETE. A single MERGE statement can only act on a single table.

Insert rows into a table

```
INSERT INTO table_name [column [,column...])]
VALUES (value [, value...]);
```

The simplest form of an insert statement inserts a single row into a single table. The following inserts a new person into the EMPLOYEES table.

```
INSERT INTO employees (emp_id, afl_id, emp_first, emp_last,
           emp_job, emp_supervisor, salary, start_date)
VALUES (18, NULL, 'Guy', 'Newberry', 'Mgr', 8, 98250,
       '07-JAN-2012');
```

The following shows a simple insert using subquery:

```
INSERT INTO aircraft_types (act_name, act_body_style,
                           act_decks, act_seats)
SELECT 'Boeing 787', act_body_style, act_decks, 300
FROM   aircraft_types
```

Update rows in a table

The following statement moves all of the employees that used to report to the employees with emp_id 9 to the new employees with emp_id 18. If no WHERE clause were supplied, all rows in the employees table would have the emp_supervisor column set to 18.

```
UPDATE employees
SET    emp_supervisor = 18
WHERE  emp_supervisor = 9;
```

Delete rows from a table

The following statement deletes from the EMPLOYEES table the employee with emp_id 9.

```
DELETE
FROM   employees
WHERE  emp_id = 9;
```

The only required portions of the DELETE syntax are a the DELETE keyword and a table name. If the above statement were only 'DELETE employees', then it would succeed and delete all rows from the employees table.

Control transactions

A transaction is composed of one or more DML statements punctuated by either a COMMIT or a ROLLBACK command. Transactions are also ended if a DDL statement is issued. This isn't technically a third method, however, since this happens because all DDL operation are preceded by an implicit COMMIT. In fact, DDL statements are also ended with an implicit COMMIT, but by that time any prior DML transactions have already been committed.

Transactions are a major part of the mechanism for ensuring the database maintains data integrity. The transaction control statements available in Oracle are:

- **COMMIT** – Used to end the current transaction and make permanent all changes performed in it.
- **ROLLBACK** -- Used to undo work done in the current transaction or to manually undo the work done by an in-doubt distributed transaction.
- **SAVEPOINT** -- Used to create a name for a specific system change number (SCN), which can be rolled back to at a later date.
- **SET TRANSACTION** – Used to establish the current transaction as read-only or read/write, establish its isolation level, assign it to a specified rollback segment, or assign a name to it.
- **SET CONSTRAINT** -- Used to specify, for a particular transaction, whether a deferrable constraint is checked following each DML statement (IMMEDIATE) or when the transaction is committed (DEFERRED).

Using DDL Statements to Create and Manage Tables

Whereas DML statements are used to manipulate data, data definition language (DDL) statements are used to make changes to the data dictionary of Oracle.   They are utilized to perform the following tasks (among others):

- Create, alter, and drop schema objects
- TRUNCATE data from a table
- Analyze information on a table, index, or cluster

Categorize the main database objects

There are over thirty different types of objects that make up the Oracle database. The list of database objects, both schema and nonschema from the 11G SQL Reference manual follows.

Schema Objects
Clusters
Constraints
Database links
Database triggers
Dimensions
External procedure libraries
Index-organized tables
Indexes
Indextypes
Java classes, resources, and sources
Materialized views
Materialized view logs
Mining models
Object tables
Object types
Object views
Operators
Packages
Sequences
Stored functions and procedures

Nonschema Objects
Contexts
Directories
Editions
Restore points
Roles
Rollback segments
Tablespaces
Users

Synonyms
Tables
Views

Not all of the available object types will be referenced on the test. A list of the objects that you're likely to see on the test along with a brief definition follows:

- **TABLE** -- The basic structure to hold user data.
- **INDEX** -- A schema object that contains an entry for each value that appears in one or more columns of a table and provides direct, fast access to rows.
- **VIEW** -- A logical table based on one or more tables or views, although it contains no data itself.
- **SEQUENCE** -- A database object from which multiple users may generate unique integers.
- **SYNONYM** -- An alternative name for another object in the database.
- **CONSTRAINT** -- A rule that restricts the values in a database column.
- **USERS** -- An account through which database users can log in to the database and which provides the basis for creating schema objects.
- **ROLES** – Container for a set of privileges that can be granted to users or to other roles.

Review the table structure

In relational databases, a table is a set of data elements organized using a model of vertical columns and horizontal rows. A table has a set number of columns, but can have any number of rows.

List the data types that are available for columns

Every value contained within the Oracle Database has a data type. The data type associates a given set of properties with the value and causes Oracle to treat the values differently. It is possible to add, subtract, or multiply two values of the NUMBER data type, but not two values of a LONG data type. Any time a table is created, each of its columns must have a data type specified. Data types define the domain of values that each column can contain. There are a number of built-in data types in Oracle and it is possible to create user-defined types that can be used as data types. The data types available for columns are:

- **VARCHAR2(n)** -- Variable-length character string of n characters or bytes.
- **NVARCHAR2(n)** -- Variable-length Unicode character string of n characters.
- **NUMBER** -- Number having optional precision and scale values.
- **FLOAT** -- A subtype of the NUMBER data type having precision but no scale.
- **LONG** -- Character data of variable length up to 2 gigabytes.
- **DATE** -- This data type contains the datetime fields YEAR, MONTH, DAY, HOUR, MINUTE, and SECOND. It does not have fractional seconds or a time zone.
- **BINARY_FLOAT** -- 32-bit floating point number.
- **BINARY_DOUBLE** -- 64-bit floating point number.
- **TIMESTAMP** -- This data type contains the datetime fields YEAR, MONTH, DAY, HOUR, MINUTE, and SECOND. It contains fractional seconds but does not have a time zone.
- **TIMESTAMP WITH TIME ZONE** -- This data type contains the datetime fields YEAR, MONTH, DAY, HOUR, MINUTE, SECOND, TIMEZONE_HOUR, and TIMEZONE_MINUTE. It has fractional seconds and an explicit time zone.
- **TIMESTAMP WITH LOCAL TIME ZONE** – Identical to TIMESTAMP WITH TIME ZONE, with the exceptions that data is normalized to the database time zone when it is stored in the database, and displayed in the current session time zone when retrieved.
- **INTERVAL DAY TO SECOND** -- Stores a period of time in days, hours, minutes, and seconds

- **INTERVAL YEAR TO MONTH** – Stored a period of time in years and months.
- **RAW(n)** -- Raw binary data of length n bytes.
- **LONG RAW** -- Raw binary data of variable length up to 2 gigabytes.
- **ROWID** -- Base 64 string representing the unique address of a row in its table.
- **UROWID** -- Base 64 string representing the logical address of a row of an index-organized table.
- **CHAR(n)** -- Fixed-length character data of length n bytes or characters.
- **NCHAR(n)** -- Fixed-length Unicode character data of length n characters.
- **CLOB** -- A character large object containing single-byte or multibyte characters.
- **NCLOB** -- A character large object containing Unicode characters.
- **BLOB** -- A binary large object.
- **BFILE** -- Contains a locator to a large binary file stored outside the database.

None of the LONG or LOB data types require (or allow) a size definition.

Create a simple table

At its most basic, an Oracle create table statement would look something like the following:

```
CREATE TABLE ocp_example (
   ocp_id              NUMBER,
   ocp_name            VARCHAR2(20),
   ocp_date            DATE);
```

The statement can be broken down into the reserved words CREATE and TABLE, followed by a name for the table, and the column list. The column list must be enclosed in parentheses, and contain column name/data type pairs separated by commas. The table name and the column names must follow Oracle naming rules (discussed next). The SQL statement will be terminated by a semicolon.

Database Object Naming Rules

Every object in the database must have a name. The names may be represented with either a quoted identifier or a nonquoted identifier. A quoted identifier is enclosed in double quotation marks ("). A nonquoted identifier uses no punctuation. Quoted identifiers allow many of the Oracle database naming rules to be circumvented. However, Oracle does not recommend doing so. A complete list of the naming conventions is available in the Oracle SQL Reference manual. A partial list follows:

- Names must be 1 to 30 bytes long with the exception of database names (8 bytes) and database links (128 bytes).
- Nonquoted identifiers cannot be Oracle SQL reserved words.
- Nonquoted identifiers must begin with an alphabetic character.
- Nonquoted identifiers can contain only alphanumeric characters from your database character set and the underscore (_), dollar sign ($), and pound sign (#).
- Nonquoted identifiers are not case sensitive. Oracle interprets them as uppercase. Quoted identifiers are case sensitive.
- Columns in the same table or view cannot have the same name. However, columns in different tables or views can have the same name.
- Within a namespace, no two objects can have the same name.

Namespaces

Namespaces are a construct that Oracle uses when locating a database object during the execution of a SQL command. In any single namespace, you may not have more than one object of the same name. Each schema in the database has its own namespace for the objects it contains.

The following schema objects share one namespace:
- Tables
- Views
- Sequences
- Private synonyms
- Stand-alone procedures
- Stand-alone stored functions

- Packages
- Materialized views
- User-defined types

The following schema objects each has its own namespace:
- Indexes
- Constraints
- Clusters
- Database triggers
- Private database links
- Dimensions

The upshot of this is that because tables and views are in the same namespace, you may not have a table and a view with the exact same name for a given schema. Likewise a table and a private synonym of the same name aren't allowed or a sequence and a view. However, indexes are in a separate namespace, so you could have a table and an index of the same name. In addition, because each schema has its own namespace, you could have tables of the same name in multiple schemas.

Explain how constraints are created at the time of table creation

Constraints are database objects that are used to restrict (constrain) the data allowed into table columns. They are essentially rules that must be met in order for a value to be acceptable. There are several different kinds of constraints available in Oracle:

Constraint types

- **PRIMARY KEY** – The primary key of a table defines a column, or set of columns that must be unique for every row of a table. To satisfy a primary key constraint, none of the column(s) making up the key may be NULL, and the combination of values in the column(s) must be unique. A table can have only a single primary key constraint defined (all other constraint types can exist multiple times in the same table).
- **UNIQUE** – A unique key defines a column or set of columns that must be unique for every row of a table. Unlike a primary key constraint, the UNIQUE constraint does not prevent NULL values in the columns(s) that make up the constraint.
- **NOT NULL** – A NOT NULL constraint prevents a table column from having NULL values. If a column with a UNIQUE constraint is also defined as NOT NULL, it will have the same restrictive behavior as a PRIMARY KEY.
- **FOREIGN KEY** – Foreign keys are also referred to as referential Integrity constraints. A foreign key constraint ties a column value in one table to a primary or unique key value in another. Values may not be inserted in the table with the reference constraint that do not exist in the referenced key.
- **CHECK** – Check constraints allow for custom conditions to be specified for a column. The conditions must evaluate to TRUE for the operation altering the column value to succeed.

Constraints in Oracle are created by one of two methods. They can be created simultaneously with the table during the CREATE TABLE statement, or they can be created on a table that already exists using the ALTER TABLE statement. There is no such thing as a 'CREATE CONSTRAINT' command. The SQL statement below creates a table with two constraints:

```
CREATE TABLE aircraft_types (
  act_id              NUMBER,
  act_name            VARCHAR2(20),
  act_body_style      VARCHAR2(10),
  act_decks           NUMBER,
  act_seats           NUMBER   NOT NULL
    CONSTRAINT ac_type_pk PRIMARY KEY (act_id)
);
```

Beyond creating the table and columns with associated data types, it contains the instructions for adding two constraints.

- The **act_seats** column has been assigned a NOT NULL constraint. If an insert to this table doesn't reference this column, or references it but attempts to add a NULL value to the column, an error will occur. Because no name was specified for the constraint, Oracle will give it a system-generated name. This is an in-line constraint definition because it is added in the same line as the column. NULL and NOT NULL constraints **must** be defined in-line during a CREATE or ALTER TABLE statement.
- The **act_id** column has been assigned a primary key constraint, and the constraint given the name 'ac_type_pk'. Oracle will create an index of the same name to enforce the primary key constraint. This constraint has been defined out-of-line.

The following is equivalent to the first SQL statement, with the primary key constraint being defined in-line:

```
CREATE TABLE aircraft_types (
  act_id                NUMBER  CONSTRAINT ac_type_pk
                                PRIMARY KEY,
  act_name              VARCHAR2(20),
  act_body_style        VARCHAR2(10),
  act_decks             NUMBER,
  act_seats             NUMBER  NOT NULL
);
```

Creating Other Schema Objects

In addition to tables, you'll need to recognize the syntax for creating views, sequences, indexes, and public synonyms.

Create simple and complex views

The base difference between simple and complex views is that a simple view selects from a single table and does not aggregate data whereas a complex view selects from more than one table and/or aggregates data. It is possible to perform DML operations against simple views. It **may** be possible to perform DML operations against a complex view, but it is dependent on the particular view.

You cannot delete or modify data via a view if either of the following is true:
- The view has aggregated data.
- The view contains the DISTINCT/UNIQUE keyword

You cannot insert data in a view if either of the above is true, or:
- There are NOT NULL columns in the table that are not selected by the view (unless these columns have a default value defined).

As a general rule you also cannot use DML on a query that contains JOINs. This rule can be circumvented if you have a key preserved table. However, key preserved tables are not an exam topic.

The following example is a simple view. It does not include the salary column from the EMPLOYEES table. Users given SELECT access on this view but *not* the base table will not be able to access employee salary information.

```
CREATE OR REPLACE VIEW employees_no_sal_v
AS
SELECT emp_first, emp_last, emp_job, start_date
FROM    employees;

view EMPLOYEES_NO_SAL_V created.
```

The following example is a complex view. By joining the AIRPORTS and AIRCRAFT_TYPES through the AIRCRAFT_FLEET table, this view allows you to easily query all of the aircraft in the fleet without having to create the joins each time.

```
CREATE OR REPLACE VIEW aircraft_fleet_v
AS
SELECT apt_name, apt_abbr, act_name, act_body_style,
act_decks, act_seats
FROM    airports apt
        INNER JOIN aircraft_fleet afl
        ON apt.apt_id = afl.apt_id
        INNER JOIN aircraft_types act
        ON act.act_id = afl.act_id;

view AIRCRAFT_FLEET_V created.
```

If any columns selected in the view are expressions, then the expression must be provided with an alias in order for a view to be created. The alias must meet normal naming convention rules. The following expands on the EMPLOYEE_NOSAL_V view created above, adding two new columns, one with the employee's full name separated by a space, and the second with their last name then the first name separated by a comma.

```
CREATE OR REPLACE VIEW employees_morenames_v
AS
SELECT emp_first, emp_last, emp_job, start_date,
        emp_first || ' ' || emp_last AS EMP_FULL_NAME,
        emp_last || ', ' || emp_first AS EMP_LAST_FIRST
FROM    employees;

view EMPLOYEES_MORENAMES_V created.
```

Another syntax for defining the view column names during creation is:

```
CREATE OR REPLACE VIEW employees_morenames_v
    (emp_first, emp_last, emp_job, start_date, emp_full_name,
emp_last_name)
AS
SELECT emp_first, emp_last, emp_job, start_date,
        emp_first || ' ' || emp_last,
        emp_last || ', ' || emp_first
FROM    employees;

view EMPLOYEES_MORENAMES_V created.
```

Retrieve data from views

Once a view exists, data is retrieved from it using SELECT statements just as if it were a table object. There are no changes to the SELECT syntax for queries against views rather than tables. It's not possible to determine from the results of a SELECT statement that the object being queried is a view rather than a table. Views are useful for a variety of purposes:

- **Reduce Complexity** -- A particularly complicated query of one or more tables in your database can be created as a view. Queries against the view then can be much simpler to create.
- **Reduce Maintenance** – Similar to the above -- if several parts of a database application will be querying one or more tables with the same basic SQL statement, creating a view that will support these queries will make maintenance easier if a change is required. Altering the view will propagate the changes to all of the SQL statements that use it.
- **Increase security** – If a table has some columns that can be accessed by one group of people and others that should not be, a view can be created without the columns on question. Access to query the view, but *not*the table can be granted to the group that should not see them.

```
SELECT emp_last_first, emp_full_name, emp_job
FROM    employees_morenames_v
ORDER BY emp_last_first;
```

EMP_LAST_FIRST	EMP_FULL_NAME	EMP_JOB
Abong, Bill	Bill Abong	VP
Alien, Alf	Alf Alien	SrDir
Aptop, Dell	Dell Aptop	Pilot
Boss, Big	Big Boss	CEO
Gun, Top	Top Gun	Pilot
Jameson, Rick	Rick Jameson	SVP
Jeckson, Janet	Janet Jeckson	VP
Jones, John	John Jones	Pilot
Kia, Noh	Noh Kia	Pilot
McCoy, Phil	Phil McCoy	Pilot
Picard, John	John Picard	Pilot
Skytalker, Luke	Luke Skytalker	Pilot
Smith, Adam	Adam Smith	CFO
Stoneflint, Fred	Fred Stoneflint	SrDir

```
Stoner, Rob          Rob Stoner          SVP
Storm, Norm          Norm Storm          Mgr
Thomas, James        James Thomas        Pilot
```

If you have the SELECT privilege for a table in another schema, and the CREATE VIEW privilege, you can create a view in your schema against the table in the other schema. However, if you may not GRANT the SELECT privilege against your view to a third user unless you have the WITH GRANT OPTION on the base table.

Create, maintain, and use sequences

Sequences are database objects from which multiple users may generate unique integers. They are often used to automatically generate primary key values. Every time a sequence number is generated, the value is incremented, <u>independent</u> of whether the transaction is committed or rolled back. If a SQL statement generates an error, it is automatically rolled back, but any sequences incremented by the call will **not** get rolled back to the value they were previously.

One user can never acquire the sequence number that was generated by another user. Once a sequence exists, the CURRVAL and NEXTVAL pseudocolumns are used to access its values. The CURRVAL pseudocolumn returns the current value of the sequence. The NEXTVAL pseudocolumn increments the sequence and returns the new value. The NEXTVAL and CURRVAL pseudocolumns cannot be used as part of a view, or in an aggregate SELECT statement.

Since sequences do nothing more than return an integer when called, there are only a few questions to be answered about them during creation and CREATE SEQUENCE is a fairly simple command:

START WITH – Specifies the first number to be returned by the sequence (default is 1).
INCREMENT BY – Specifies the integer that will be added to the sequence value each time it is called. This number can be positive or negative (default is 1).
MINVALUE – the lowest value that will be returned by the sequence (default is NOMAXVALUE).

MAXVALUE – The highest value that will be returned by the sequence (default is NOMINVALUE).
CYCLE – Determines whether the sequence will cycle through the same set of numbers continuously or not (default is NOCYCLE).
CACHE – Determines whether or not the sequence will cache values in memory for faster retrieval and how many (default is CACHE 20). NOCACHE will turn off sequence caching entirely.

A sequence created with all default values will start at one, and increment by 1 with no maximum value and utilize a cache of 20 values). To create a sequence that stops at a predefined limit, specify a value for the MAXVALUE or MINVALUE parameters (for ascending/descending sequences respectively) and add NOCYCLE. Once the sequence has reached its limit, any further calls to NEXTVAL generate an error.

To create a sequence that restarts after reaching a predefined limit, specify the MAXVALUE or MINVALUE parameters for ascending/descending sequences, a START WITH value, and CYCLE. When the sequence hits either the MAXVALUE or MINVALUE, the next call to NEXTVAL will return the START WITH value.

The following example creates a sequence called SEQ_EMP_ID that starts with the number 18, increments by one each time the NEXTVAL pseudocolumn is referenced, and does not cache any values.

```
CREATE SEQUENCE seq_emp_id
START WITH 18
INCREMENT BY 1
NOCACHE;

sequence SEQ_EMP_ID created.
```

Once created, we can pull the next number from the sequence as follows:

```
SELECT seq_emp_id.nextval FROM dual;

NEXTVAL
-------
     18
```

If we were to make the above call a second time, it would return the value 19. However, we can pull the current sequence value without causing it to increment by usein thr CURRVAL pseudocolumn:

```
SELECT seq_emp_id.currval FROM dual;

CURRVAL
-------
     18
```

Create and maintain indexes

Indexes contain an entry for each value that is stored in the indexed column(s) of the table. Each index entry contains a locator to the block(s) in the data file containing the row(s) with that value and provide direct, fast access to them. Tables can have multiple indexes created on them. The tradeoffs involved in creating multiple indexes on the same table are outside the scope of this test. Any DML statement that includes an indexed column in a WHERE clause <u>might</u> see a performance benefit. The uncertainty lies in the fact that the Oracle Cost Based Optimizer may or may not choose to make use of the index.

Oracle supports several types of index:
- **Normal indexes** -- The default index type in Oracle is a B-tree index.
- **Bitmap indexes** -- Store the ROWID values associated with a key value as a bitmap. A bitmap index cannot be UNIQUE.
- **Partitioned indexes** -- Consist of partitions containing an entry for each value that appears in the indexed column(s) of the table.
- **Function-based indexes** – Store expressions based on column data rather than the column data itself. They enable you to construct queries that filter by an expression and get the performance benefit of an index.

When a primary key or unique constraint is added to a table, and there is not already an appropriate unique index on the column(s) the constraint is for, an index will be added to the table to enforce the constraint. We can find the index created earlier for the aircraft_types primary key by querying the USER_INDEXES view:

```
SELECT table_name, index_name
FROM   user_indexes
WHERE  table_name = 'AIRCRAFT_TYPES';

TABLE_NAME                  INDEX_NAME
----------------------      -------------
AIRCRAFT_TYPES              SYS_C006988
```

When creating indexes manually via the CREATE INDEX command, you can index a single column:

```
CREATE INDEX emp_last_ndx
ON employees (emp_last);

index EMP_LAST_NDX created.
```

You can also create a single index that contains multiple columns:

```
CREATE INDEX emp_last_first_ndx
ON employees (emp_last, emp_first);

index EMP_LAST_FIRST_NDX created.
```

Whenever a DML query includes one or more indexed columns in the WHERE clause, the Oracle Cost Based Optimizer has to decide whether or not making use of the index will improve the performance of the operation. The optimizer uses table statistics to try to determine what percentage of rows in the table will be returned by the query. If the answer is most (or all) of the rows in the table, then skipping the index in favor of a full-table scan is likely to be the better option from a performance standpoint. The full scope of the CBO decision-making process is much more complex, but this is a significant part of the decision on using indexes. Indexes are never used when the comparison being performed is '!=', 'NOT IN', or 'IS NULL' or if the column being compared is in a function and the index is not a function-based index (using the same function as is in the WHERE clause).

Oracle maintains indexes automatically. There is no command that you must issue to account for a row being added or deleted, or an indexed value being changed. Every time a table change is made that affects an indexed value, Oracle performs the necessary updates to all affected indexes on that table. The automated work is part of the downside to having multiple indexes on a given table. Multiple indexes **might** improve performance for selects, but they **will** create overhead that reduces performance for inserts, updates and deletes.

The only manual performance operation that you might perform on an index is a rebuild. Index rebuilds can sometimes reduce the size and improve the performance characteristics for an index that has had a lot of data changes since the index was built (or last rebuilt).

```
ALTER INDEX emp_last_first_ndx REBUILD;

index EMP_LAST_FIRST_NDX altered.
```

If you decide that an index is not being used or if you want to replace it with an index created in a different fashion, you can remove it from the data dictionary with the DROP INDEX command. If a table with indexes is dropped, all of the associated indexes will be dropped automatically.

```
DROP INDEX emp_last_first_ndx;

index EMP_LAST_FIRST_NDX dropped.
```

Create private and public synonyms

A SYNONYM in Oracle is a data dictionary object that is an alternate name for a different data dictionary object. It has **no** connection to the object that it points to, and indeed a SYNONYM can be created for a non-existent object. If an object that a synonym points to is dropped, the synonym itself is unchanged. The reverse is also true – dropping a synonym has no effect on the object it pointed to.

Public synonyms are useful for separating the fully-qualified names of databases objects from the names used to reference them in database applications. For example, assume you had a developer who created an application in the schema JJONES with all tables, procedures, etc. in there. If he left the company, moving those objects out of the schema would likely require a significant amount of development to point everything to their new location. Public synonyms can be used to either prevent problems like this from occurring or solve them after the fact.

There are two broad classes of synonyms:
- **PRIVATE** – Private synonyms are schema objects. They are used only for calls that originate in the schema in which they are created.
- **PUBLIC** – Public synonyms are non-schema objects. They are available to all database users.

Once a synonym exists, it can be used as part of a SQL statement. As mentioned above, the synonym doesn't verify the destination object exists or provide any rights to it if it does. If a SELECT statement against the base table will fail, then a SELECT statement against a synonym pointing to that table will fail as well. All that really happens inside Oracle when a synonym is used is that Oracle replaces one identifier with the other before executing the SQL. In the below example, a private synonym named VIEW_EMPLOYEES is created for the EMPLOYEES_MORENAMES_V view.

```
CREATE OR REPLACE SYNONYM view_employees FOR
employees_morenames_v;

synonym VIEW_EMPLOYEES created.
```

Executing a DESCRIBE against the new synonym shows the structure of the EMPLOYEES_MORENAMES_V view.

```
DESC view_employees

Name            Null Type
--------------- ---- ------------
EMP_FIRST            VARCHAR2(10)
EMP_LAST            VARCHAR2(10)
EMP_JOB            VARCHAR2(10)
START_DATE            DATE
EMP_FULL_NAME            VARCHAR2(21)
EMP_LAST_FIRST            VARCHAR2(22)
```

In the below example, a public synonym named VIEW_EMPLOYEES is created for the EMPLOYEES_NO_SAL_V view.

```
CREATE OR REPLACE PUBLIC SYNONYM view_employees FOR
employees_no_sal_v;

public synonym VIEW_EMPLOYEES created.
```

The statement succeeds even though a private synonym of that name already exists. This is because public and private synonyms don't share the same namespace. However, a DESCRIBE against the new synonym still shows the structure of the EMPLOYEES_MORENAMES_V view.

```
DESC view_employees
Name              Null  Type
-------------     ----  ------------
EMP_FIRST               VARCHAR2(10)
EMP_LAST                VARCHAR2(10)
EMP_JOB                 VARCHAR2(10)
START_DATE              DATE
EMP_FULL_NAME           VARCHAR2(21)
EMP_LAST_FIRST          VARCHAR2(22)
```

This is because when Oracle is resolving an object, it will look in the current schema first. If you have a private synonym named VIEW_EMPLOYEES in your schema pointing to object A, and there is a public synonym named VIEW_EMPLOYEES that points to object B, then a query from inside your schema against the VIEW_EMPLOYEES synonym will pull results from object A. If the private synonym created earlier is dropped, then executing a DESCRIBE against VIEW_EMPLOYEES will use the public synonym and display the structure of the EMPLOYEES_NO_SAL_V view.

```
DROP SYNONYM view_employees;

synonym VIEW_EMPLOYEES dropped.

DESC view_employees

Name          Null  Type
----------    ----  ------------
EMP_FIRST           VARCHAR2(10)
EMP_LAST            VARCHAR2(10)
EMP_JOB             VARCHAR2(10)
START_DATE          DATE
```

The syntax to DROP a private synonym follows. Since it is a schema object, if you are not the owner of the synonym, you must prefix it with a schema name (and also have the DROP ANY SYNONYM privilege).

```
DROP SYNONYM view_employees;
```

The syntax to DROP a public synonym follows. PUBLIC synonyms are not associated with a schema and will never have a schema prefix.

```
DROP PUBLIC SYNONYM view_employees;
```

Managing Objects with Data Dictionary Views

The data dictionary of Oracle contains every single piece of information about the tables, indexes, views, synonyms, procedures, and every other type of object that exists in the database. If you know where to look (and have sufficient privileges), it is possible to locate the SQL to recreate every object in the system. The data dictionary also contains usage information, statistics about the data, and information about the performance of the database. Luckily, ninety percent of what can be done with the data dictionary is outside the scope of this test so it can be ignored in this guide.

Use the data dictionary views to research data on your objects

All of the data dictionary tables are owned by the SYS account, and tend to have very cryptic names. Few accounts have access to view these tables at all. Querying the tables directly is not recommended and in all but a vanishingly small number of exceptions not worthwhile. The vast majority of the data you need from the data dictionary can be retrieved from views created specifically for the purpose of exposing the information required by users and administrators. A significant number of these views come with one of three prefixes:

- **DBA_** -- These views show data dictionary objects across all schemas. The views are intended to be used by people with Database Administrator-level privileges.
- **ALL_** -- These views show data dictionary objects across multiple schemas. The objects shown are filtered based on object level privileges, however. Objects in schemas other than the user querying the view will only be shown if the user has privileges on the object in the other schema.
- **USER_** – These views show only data dictionary objects that exist in the schema that is performing the query. The USER views lack the OWNER column that exists in the DBA_ and ALL_ views, since the information is redundant.

The majority of the views outside the above three contain performance statistics:

- **V$** -- Dynamic performance views for the local database
- **GV$** -- Global dynamic performance views for multiple instances when utilizing Real Application Clusters.

It's obviously not possible in this book to detail all of the available views. However, some of the more useful views on non-schema objects are:

- **DBA_USERS** -- Information about all users of the database.
- **DICTIONARY** -- Description of data dictionary tables and views.
- **DICT_COLUMNS** -- Description of columns in data dictionary tables and views.
- **GLOBAL_NAME** – Displays the global database name.
- **NLS_DATABASE_PARAMETERS** -- Permanent NLS parameters of the database.
- **SESSION_PRIVS** – Displays all system privileges available in the current session.

Likewise some of the more useful views on schema objects are: (USER views shown, there are DBA and ALL equivalents)

- **USER_INDEXES** -- Describes all indexes in the current schema.
- **USER_IND_COLUMNS** -- Describes the columns of indexes on all tables in the current schema.
- **USER_SEQUENCES** -- Describes all sequences in the current schema.
- **USER_SYNONYMS** -- Describes all synonyms in the current schema.
- **USER_SYS_PRIVS** -- Describes system privileges granted to the current user.
- **USER_TAB_COLUMNS** -- Describes columns of all tables, views, and clusters in the current schema.
- **USER_TAB_PRIVS** -- Describes all object grants in the current schema.
- **USER_TABLES** -- Describes all relational tables in the current schema.
- **USER_OBJECTS** -- Describes all objects in the current schema.

The dynamic performance views are extremely useful for getting information about your database. They display information about your database in real time. The views themselves actually have names that begin with **V_$**, but they each have matching public synonyms that start with **V$**. When using these views, you should be aware that Oracle does not recommend complex queries against them, with or without joins. Because of the dynamic nature of the views, Oracle cannot guarantee read consistency when anything other than simple single-view queries are executed against them. Some of the V$ views are:

- **V$DATABASE** -- This view lets you access information about the database (such as archivelog status).
- **V$DATAFILE** -- This view contains an entry for each datafile of the database.
- **V$NLS_PARAMETERS** -- The NLS parameters that are in effect for the session querying this view.
- **V$PARAMETER** -- Lists the name-value pairs of the init.ora file (or their default, if not in the init.ora).
- **V$SQLTEXT_WITH_NEWLINES** -- This view can be used to construct the entire text for each session's actual SQL statement.
- **V$VERSION** -- Use this view to find out the specific version of the database components.

Query various data dictionary views

The USER_TABLES view can provide you with more information about a table than you ever wanted to know. The columns below are just a fraction of the ones available.

```
SELECT table_name, status, pct_free, pct_used,
       num_rows, blocks
FROM   user_tables
WHERE  table_name = 'AIRPORTS';

TABLE_NAME    STATUS    PCT_FREE PCT_USED NUM_ROWS BLOCKS
------------- -------- --------- --------- -------- ------
AIRPORTS      VALID           10        40        5      1
```

The V$VERSION view is useful for determining exactly which versions of Oracle software the current database is running.

```
SELECT *
FROM   v$version;

BANNER
----------------------------------------------------------
Oracle Database 11g Express Edition Release 11.2.0.2.0 -
Production
PL/SQL Release 11.2.0.2.0 - Production
CORE    11.2.0.2.0  Production
TNS for 32-bit Windows: Version 11.2.0.2.0 - Production
NLSRTL Version 11.2.0.2.0 - Production
```

The DICTIONARY view is an excellent starting point for learning about the data dictionary objects available. The COMMENTS field gives a brief description of the vast majority of objects available.

```
SELECT *
FROM   dictionary
WHERE  table_name LIKE 'USER_COL%'

TABLE_NAME              COMMENTS
----------------------- ------------------------------------
USER_COLL_TYPES         Description of the user's own named
                          collection types
USER_COL_COMMENTS       Comments on columns of user's tables
                          and views
USER_COL_PENDING_STATS  Pending statistics of tables,
                          partitions, and subpartitions
USER_COL_PRIVS_MADE     All grants on columns of objects
                          owned by the user
USER_COL_PRIVS_RECD     Grants on columns for which the
                          user is the grantee
```

Controlling User Access

In order for a RDBMS to be a viable platform for enterprise databases, the data must secure. The sum total of the data within it should not be freely available to anyone that can log in to the database. Oracle maintains security within the database through the use of user privileges. The two most common means of controlling user privileges are:

- Granting and revoking privileges to individual users or groups of users.
- Creating a database role and assigning privileges to it. A role is a named database object to which you grant related privileges. You can then grant that role (and all associated privileges) to users or to other roles.

A third means is through the use of secure application roles. However, that is outside the scope of the test.

Differentiate system privileges from object privileges

There are two broad classes of privileges that can be granted to a user or role:

- **System Privileges** – Provide the ability to perform a task that has a scope beyond that of a single database object. Many the system privileges have a scope of the entire database, for example ALTER USER or CREATE ROLLBACK SEGMENT. Others have a scope that is just for the schema of the user who has been granted the privilege, for example CREATE TABLE or CREATE PROCEDURE.
- **Object Privileges** – Provide the ability to perform a task on a specific database object. For example, GRANT SELECT ON employees.

Some examples of System Privileges are:
- **CREATE TABLE** -- Create a table in the grantee's schema.
- **CREATE ANY TABLE** -- Create a table in any schema.
- **ALTER ANY TABLE** -- Alter any table or view in any schema.
- **DELETE ANY TABLE** -- Delete rows from tables in any schema.
- **DROP ANY TABLE** -- Drop (or truncate) tables in any schema.
- **INSERT ANY TABLE** -- Insert rows into tables in any schema.
- **CREATE ANY INDEX** Create an index on any table in any schema.
- **ALTER ANY INDEX** Alter indexes in any schema.

Some examples of Object Privileges are:
- **ALTER** – Right to use ALTER TABLE to change a given table.
- **INDEX** – Right to use the CREATE INDEX command on a given table.
- **INSERT** – Right to INSERT new rows into a given table.
- **SELECT** – Right to SELECT data from a given table.
- **UPDATE** – Right to UPDATE data in a given table.
- **DELETE** – Right to use DELETE rows from a given table.

PUBLIC

If there is a requirement that every database user have a given privilege, its possible to grant that privilege to PUBLIC. After granting a privilege to PUBLIC, the privilege is freely available to every single database user without exception. This must always be used with caution, especially when dealing with system privileges. System grants to PUBLIC should be avoided as a general rule.

ANY keyword

A significant percentage of system privileges have two similar commands, with and without the ANY keyword (i.e. CREATE TABLE vs CREATE ANY TABLE). The ANY keyword means that the grant is not schema-specific. When a user is granted CREATE TABLE, they are able to create tables in their own schema. However, when granted CREATE ANY TABLE, they can create tables in any user's schema. The ANY keyword makes the privilege much less restrictive and therefore much more dangerous.

WITH ADMIN OPTION

System privileges may optionally be made using the WITH ADMIN option (i.e. GRANT ALTER ANY TABLE WITH ADMIN OPTION). This option allows the user granted this privilege to grant it to other users in turn. In fact, they can grant the privilege to a third user 'WITH ADMIN OPTION' who could in turn grant it to a fourth and so on. If the system privilege is later revoked from a user who was given the admin option, any grants they made of this system privilege are <u>not</u> revoked. The revoke of system privileges **does not** cascade.

WITH GRANT OPTION

Object privileges have a similar clause called the WITH GRANT OPTION. When an object privilege is granted to a user with this option, that user can grant the object privilege to other users. One distinct difference between the two is that if the privilege is revoked from a user given the WITH GRANT OPTION, any privileges that the user granted are also revoked. The revoke of object privileges **does** cascade.

Grant privileges on tables

In order to access tables that are owned by another schema, you must have been granted access to do so. This might be through a system privilege such as SELECT ANY TABLE, or by a grant on the table itself by the schema owner, or a schema that has privileges that allow it to grant the required access. Until a privilege has been granted, Oracle will treat attempts to SELECT from it as if the table does not even exist.

```
SELECT *
FROM    hr.regions;

ORA-00942: table or view does not exist
00942. 00000 -  "table or view does not exist"
*Cause:
*Action:
```

If the SELECT privilege is granted to the querying schema, then the above statement will succeed:

```
GRANT SELECT ON hr.regions TO ocpguru;

GRANT succeeded.

SELECT *
FROM   hr.regions;

REGION_ID REGION_NAME
--------- ------------------------
        1 Europe
        2 Americas
        3 Asia
        4 Middle East and Africa
```

To remove a privilege that has been granted, the REVOKE statement is required:

```
REVOKE SELECT ON hr.regions FROM ocpguru;

REVOKE succeeded.
```

View privileges in the data dictionary

There are numerous views in the data dictionary that allow you to determine which rights are granted to users or roles. Listed below are the views specific to the current schema. Most of these views have DBA_ and ALL_ variants that show privileges for multiple schemas.

- **USER_SYS_PRIVS** -- Describes system privileges granted to the current user.
- **USER_ROLE_PRIVS** -- Describes the roles granted to the current user.
- **USER_COL_PRIVS** -- Describes the column object grants for which the current user is the object owner, grantor, or grantee.
- **USER_COL_PRIVS_MADE** -- Describes the column object grants for which the current user is the object owner.
- **USER_COL_PRIVS_RECD** -- Describes the column object grants for which the current user is the grantee.

- **USER_TAB_PRIVS** -- Describes the object grants for which the current user is the object owner, grantor, or grantee.
- **USER_TAB_PRIVS_MADE** -- Describes the object grants for which the current user is the object owner.
- **USER_TAB_PRIVS_RECD** -- Describes the object grants for which the current user is the grantee.

The USER_TAB_PRIVS table shows all table privileges that have been granted to the current schema:

```
SELECT grantee, table_name, grantor, privilege, grantable
FROM   user_tab_privs;

GRANTEE OWNER TABLE_NAME  GRANTOR PRIVILEGE GRANTABLE
------- ----- ----------- ------- --------- ---------
OCPGURU HR    DEPARTMENTS HR      DELETE    NO
OCPGURU HR    DEPARTMENTS HR      UPDATE    NO
OCPGURU HR    DEPARTMENTS HR      SELECT    NO
```

The USER_TAB_PRIVS_MADE table shows all table privileges that have been granted to the current schema:

```
SELECT * FROM user_tab_privs_made;

no rows selected


GRANT SELECT ON airports TO hr;

GRANT succeeded.


SELECT * FROM user_tab_privs_made;

GRANTEE TABLE_NAME GRANTOR PRIVILEGE GRANTABLE HIERARCHY
------- ---------- ------- --------- --------- ---------
HR      AIRPORTS   OCPGURU SELECT    NO        NO
```

Grant roles

Both system and object privileges can be granted to roles, and those roles subsequently granted to users. Roles are useful for quickly and easily granting multiple permissions to users. There are also a number of roles that have been pre-defined by Oracle. You can grant these roles to users if you wish. However, Oracle recommends creating your own roles that contain only the privileges pertaining to your requirements so that you have more control.   Oracle has been known to change the privileges in pre-defined roles. They did so with the CONNECT role, which originally had nine privileges, but now only has the CREATE SESSION privilege. Roles can contains system privileges or object privileges or both.

```
CREATE ROLE hr_authority;
role HR_AUTHORITY created.

GRANT SELECT ON employees TO hr_authority;
GRANT succeeded.

GRANT UPDATE ON employees TO hr_authority;
GRANT succeeded.

GRANT DELETE ON employees TO hr_authority;
GRANT succeeded.

GRANT hr_authority to jjones;
GRANT succeeded.
```

Distinguish between privileges and roles

A role is a container for a set of privileges. It is not in and of itself a privilege. When created, a new role contains no privileges and granting it to a user would confer no additional rights within the database. Once privileges have been added to a role and the role granted to a user, the user can then enable it and exercise the privileges granted by it.

Privileges granted to a schema are part of that schema even when the user is not logged in to the database. By contrast, the privileges a schema has from a role are only in effect while the user has an open database session (and even then, it is possible to disable a role for a given session).

Although this is outside the scope of the test, I'll note that one consequence of roles being only in effect during a session is that it is not possible to created stored PL/SQL objects that require a privilege granted to a schema via a role. For example, if you had the SELECT privilege on the EMPLOYEES table through a role, you would not be able to create a stored procedure that had a cursor referencing the table (although you could make use of such a cursor in an anonymous PL/SQL block). Since stored PL/SQL procedures might be used when a user is not currently logged into the database, either by another user or through a scheduled job, the rights required by the procedure must be persistent.

Managing Schema Objects

The exam will verify your ability to perform a variety of maintenance tasks on schema objects.

Add constraints

Earlier in this guide there were examples of constraints being generated at the time of table creation. You can also add constraints to a table after it has been created using the ALTER TABLE statement. To add a NOT NULL constraint to a column in an existing table, the command would be of the form:

```
ALTER TABLE employees MODIFY (last_name NOT NULL);

table EMPLOYEES altered.
```

This would add a unnamed NOT NULL constraint to the LAST_NAME column. Note that this statement would fail if any of the rows in column LAST_NAME contains a NULL at the time of the statement.

```
CREATE UNIQUE INDEX airport_codes_uk ON airports (apt_abbr);
unique index AIRPORT_CODES_UK created.

ALTER TABLE airports MODIFY (apt_abbr CONSTRAINT
airport_codes_uk
                         UNIQUE USING INDEX
airport_codes_uk);
table AIRPORTS altered.
```

This would add a UNIQUE constraint called AIRPORT_CODES_UK to the APT_ABBR column and use the AIRPORT_CODES_UK index that had already been created. Note that this statement would fail if any of the rows in column ABBR contain duplicates at the time of the statement.

Adding any constraint to a table with data will fail if the data in the table will violate the constraint unless the constraint is created with the NOVALIDATE option (discussed shortly).

When creating a constraint, you can specify how and when Oracle should enforce it. The DEFERABLE clause indicated whether it is possible to delay the enforcement of the constraint to a later time. The options are deferrable and not deferrable. Once set, they cannot be changed without dropping and recreating the constraint.

- **NOT DEFERRABLE** -- Indicates that it is not possible to use the SET CONSTRAINT[S] clause to defer checking of this constraint until the transaction is committed. The checking of a NOT DEFERRABLE constraint can **never** be deferred to the end of the transaction. This is the default.
- **DEFERRABLE** -- Indicate that it is possible to use the SET CONSTRAINT[S] clause to defer checking of this constraint until a COMMIT statement is submitted. If the constraint check fails, then the database returns an error and the transaction is rolled back.

Closely related to the deferrable option is the INITIALLY clause. It establishes the default checking behavior for DEFERRABLE constraints. The INITIALLY setting can be overridden by a subsequent transaction using the SET CONSTRAINT(S) statement.

- **INITIALLY IMMEDIATE** -- Indicates that Oracle should check the constraint at the end of each subsequent SQL statement. This is the default.
- **INITIALLY DEFERRED** -- Indicates that Oracle should check this constraint at the end of subsequent transactions. This is only valid if the constraint has been declared as DEFERRABLE.

You can also specify whether the constraint is enabled at creation or not, and whether the data will be validated. The four variations are:

- **ENABLE VALIDATE** -- Specifies that the constraint will be enabled at creation and all old and new data complies with the constraint. This option guarantees that all data is and will continue to be valid. If any row in the table violates the integrity constraint, then the constraint remains disabled and Oracle returns an error. Constraints are enabled by default.

- **ENABLE NOVALIDATE** – Enables the constraint but does not check pre-existing data. It ensures that all new DML operations on the constrained data comply with the constraint. If you enable a constraint but specify neither VALIDATE nor NOVALIDATE, then the default is VALIDATE.
- **DISABLE VALIDATE** – This option disables the constraint and drops the related index, but keeps the constraint valid.
- **DISABLE NOVALIDATE** – This option signifies that Oracle will make no effort to maintain the constraint (because it is disabled) and cannot guarantee that the constraint is true (because it is not being validated). If you disable a constraint but specify neither VALIDATE nor NOVALIDATE, the default is NOVALIDATE. If you disable a unique or primary key constraint that is using a unique index, then the unique index will be dropped.

Removing Constraints

The following statement drops the primary key of the AIRPORTS table.

```
ALTER TABLE airports
DROP PRIMARY KEY CASCADE;

table AIRPORTS altered.
```

You could alternately use the name of the PRIMARY KEY constraint to drop it with the following syntax:

```
ALTER TABLE airports
DROP CONSTRAINT airports_pk CASCADE;

table AIRPORTS altered.
```

The CASCADE clause indicated that Oracle should also drop any foreign keys that reference the primary key. If the CASCADE option had not been included, and any foreign key constraints referenced this key, then the statement would fail.

The following statement drops the unique key of the AIRPORTS table for the APT_ABBR column.

```
ALTER TABLE airports
DROP UNIQUE (apt_abbr);

table AIRPORTS altered.
```

You could alternately use the name of the UNIQUE KEY constraint to drop it with the following syntax:

```
ALTER TABLE airports
DROP CONSTRAINT airport_codes_uk;

table AIRPORTS altered.
```

Create indexes

The team working on the list of objectives for this exam apparently wanted to ensure index creation was fully covered. Under 'Creating Other Schema Objects' is the objective: 'Create and Maintain Indexes'. Under 'Managing Schema Objects' is the current objective: 'Create Indexes', and the objective following this one is 'Create indexes using the CREATE TABLE statement'. The only indexes that get generated on table creation are those for constraints. Since this objective is shoehorned between that and the 'Add Constraints' objective, the smart money says that their intent for this section was the creation of indexes when adding a constraint using the ALTER TABLE statement.

The two constraints that make use of indexes for enforcement are PRIMARY KEY and UNIQUE constraints. If you add one of these two constraints to a table then an index will be required for the constraint to create successfully. When defining the state of the constraint, you can specify an existing index for Oracle to use for enforcement, or you can instruct Oracle to create a new index, or neither. The three possible options are:

- If you specify USING schema.index, then Oracle attempts to use the specified index. If Oracle cannot find the index or cannot use the index to enforce the constraint an error will be returned.
- If you specify the create_index_statement, then Oracle attempts to create the index and use it to enforce the constraint. If Oracle cannot create the index or cannot use the index to enforce the constraint, then an error is returned.
- If you neither specify an existing index nor create a new index, then Oracle creates the index automatically and generates a unique (and ugly) name for the new index.

Earlier, we added a UNIQUE constraint to the airports table with this statement:

```
ALTER TABLE airports MODIFY (apt_abbr
  CONSTRAINT airport_codes_uk
  UNIQUE USING INDEX airport_codes_uk);
```

An alternate syntax that would have identical results is:

```
ALTER TABLE airports
  ADD CONSTRAINT airport_codes_uk
  UNIQUE (apt_abbr) USING INDEX airport_codes_uk;
```

If a unique index does not already exist on AIRPORTS.APT_ABBR, then one can be created explicitly as part of the ALTER TABLE statement that creates the constraint:

```
ALTER TABLE airports
  ADD CONSTRAINT airport_codes_uk
  UNIQUE (apt_abbr) USING INDEX
  (CREATE UNIQUE INDEX apt_abbr_uk
   ON airports(apt_abbr));
```

If you add a UNIQUE constraint and provide a constraint name but no USING clause, an index with the same name as the constraint will be created automatically.

```
ALTER TABLE airports
  ADD CONSTRAINT airport_codes_uk
```

```
UNIQUE (apt_abbr);
```

If you add a UNIQUE constraint and provide no constraint name or USING clause, and no index exists that could be used to enforce the constraint, an index will be created automatically. The index and the constraint will be given a system-generated name.

```
ALTER TABLE airports
  ADD UNIQUE (apt_abbr);

table AIRPORTS altered.

SELECT index_name, index_type, uniqueness
FROM    user_indexes
WHERE   table_name = 'AIRPORTS';

INDEX_NAME      INDEX_TYPE      UNIQUENESS
-------------   -------------   ----------
SYS_C007010     NORMAL          UNIQUE
```

Create indexes using the CREATE TABLE statement

The same guidelines mentioned above for adding constraints via the ALTER TABLE command are in effect when PRIMARY KEY or UNIQUE constraints are included in the CREATE TABLE statement. They must have an index in place if the constraints are to be enforced. The same three options available for adding a constraint via the ALTER TABLE statement are in effect for the CREATE TABLE statement. The following example creates a table with two constraints. The first uses a system-generated index and the second specifically creates an index to enforce the constraint:

```
CREATE TABLE constraint_test (
col1     NUMBER       UNIQUE,
col2     VARCHAR2(10) UNIQUE USING INDEX
       (CREATE UNIQUE INDEX col2_ndx
        ON constraint_test(col2)));

table CONSTRAINT_TEST created.
```

Creating function-based indexes

Function-based indexes consist of expressions rather than data that is stored in a database table. Prior to the addition of function-based indexes, it was not possible to have an indexed search when the column data in the WHERE clause was modified in any way. As an example, you might want to have all searches against employee names be case-insensitive. It's always been possible to make a query that did this:

```
SELECT emp_first, emp_last, emp_job
FROM    employees
WHERE   UPPER(emp_last) = 'GUN';

EMP_FIRST  EMP_LAST   EMP_JOB
---------- ---------- ----------
Top        Gun        Pilot
```

However, applying the UPPER function to the emp_last_name column prevents the use of a standard index on that column. However, with function-based indexes, you can create an index specifically on UPPER(emp_last_name) and at that point, the above query will be able to make use of an index scan.

```
CREATE INDEX emp_upper_last_fbndx
ON employees(UPPER(emp_last));

index EMP_UPPER_LAST_FBNDX created.
```

Drop columns and set column UNUSED

The DROP option of the ALTER TABLE statement allows you to permanently remove one or more columns from a table. If a column is not being utilized, dropping it will free up space and potentially improve performance. There are two variants of the drop column syntax:

```
ALTER TABLE constraint_test
DROP COLUMN col2;

ALTER TABLE constraint_test
DROP (col2);
```

The first variant allows you to drop a single column from a table. The second variant has the capability to drop multiple columns at once. To drop more than one column, you would list them all in the parentheses, separated by commas. It is possible to drop all but one column of the table (a table cannot exist with zero columns).

If dropping a column that is referenced by a foreign key constraint, you would need to add the CASCADE CONSTRAINTS clause to the statement. This would cause any associated foreign key constraints to be dropped at the same time as the column.

```
ALTER TABLE constraint_test
DROP COLUMN col2 CASCADE CONSTRAINTS;
```

There is a second approach to removing a column from a table. You may use the SET UNUSED clause of the ALTER TABLE statement to make a column **permanently** unusable. SET UNUSED is simply a precursor to dropping the column – it's not a halfway measure that you can change back at some point in the future. In all ways except for recovering the space used by the column, SET UNUSED is equivalent to DROP COLUMN in its behavior. The only reason to set a column unused rather than dropping is if it is important that the column be made inaccessible immediately, but it's not feasible to take the performance hit required when dropping a column. For example, dropping a column of a multi-million row table would cause a good bit of disk and database activity as the entire table is updated. The SET UNUSED command, by contrast, simply updates the data dictionary and so is instant and low impact. Just as with the DROP option, there are two variants of SET UNUSED that allow you to set one column unused or multiple columns

```
ALTER TABLE constraint_test
SET UNUSED COLUMN col2;
```

```
ALTER TABLE constraint_test
SET UNUSED (col2);
```

At some future point, presumably at a time of low usage, the column will be dropped using the DROP UNUSED COLUMNS clause. Until the unused column(s) have been dropped, the column data continues to be physically present in the table (albeit completely inaccessible). The command to drop columns in a table that have been marked unused is:

```
ALTER TABLE constraint_test
DROP UNUSED COLUMNS;
```

Perform FLASHBACK operations

With 11G, Oracle introduced a number of features under the umbrella of flashback functionality. The capabilities are implemented and accessed via a number of different methods. The common factor between them is that all of them allow you to access data and or database objects as they existed at an earlier point in time without having to perform media recovery of the database. Capabilities of Oracle Flashback include:

- Performing queries that return past data.
- Performing queries that return metadata with a history of changes to the database.
- Recover tables or rows to a previous point in time.
- Automatically create an archive of transactional data changes.
- Roll back a transaction and its dependent transactions.

The scope of flashback capabilities is significant and many of the functions are linked more closely to recovery and DBA level operations than to SQL queries. In this guide, we'll cover the three aspects most likely to appear on the test: Flashback Query, Flashback Version Query, and Flashback Transaction Query.

Oracle Flashback Query

Flashback Query is used to retrieve data for a time in the past that is specified using the AS OF clause in a SELECT statement. When the AS OF clause is included in a query and references a past time through a timestamp or System Change Number (SCN), Oracle returns committed data that existed in the database at that point in time. You can use this to recover lost data or reverse committed changes. You can also use the results to compare current data with past data.

The example below demonstrates recovery of an accidentally deleted row using Oracle Flashback Query:

```
DELETE FROM employees
WHERE   emp_last = 'Stoneflint';

1 rows deleted.


SELECT *
FROM    employees
WHERE emp_last = 'Stoneflint';

no rows selected


SELECT emp_id, emp_first, emp_last, emp_job, salary
FROM    employees
  AS OF TIMESTAMP
    TO_TIMESTAMP('29-MAR-12 11.00.00 PM',
                 'DD-MON-YY HH:MI:SS AM')
     WHERE emp_last = 'Stoneflint';

EMP_ID EMP_FIRST EMP_LAST    EMP_JOB SALARY
------ --------- ---------- ------- ------
     7 Fred      Stoneflint SrDir    111500


INSERT INTO employees
(SELECT *
FROM    employees
  AS OF TIMESTAMP
    TO_TIMESTAMP('29-MAR-12 11.00.00 PM',
                 'DD-MON-YY HH:MI:SS AM')
     WHERE emp_last = 'Stoneflint');

1 rows inserted.
```

```
SELECT emp_id, emp_first, emp_last, emp_job, salary
FROM    employees
WHERE emp_last = 'Stoneflint';

EMP_ID EMP_FIRST EMP_LAST   EMP_JOB SALARY
------ --------- ---------- ------- -------
     7     Fred  Stoneflint SrDir    111500
```

When utilizing a timestamp in the AS OF clause, Oracle converts the timestamp to an SCN within a 3-second range. If you need to have absolute accuracy on the query, you can use an SCN in the AS OF query instead of a timestamp. If you specify SCN, then the supplied expression must evaluate to a number.

```
SELECT emp_id, emp_first, emp_last, emp_job, salary
FROM    employees
  AS OF SCN 392611
WHERE emp_last = 'Stoneflint';

EMP_ID EMP_FIRST EMP_LAST   EMP_JOB SALARY
------ --------- ---------- ------- -------
     7 Fred      Stoneflint SrDir    111500
```

It's possible to specify a relative time when using the AS OF clause. The example below creates a view that will always return data as it existed three hours in the past.

```
CREATE VIEW employees_minus3_hours_v AS
SELECT * FROM employees
AS OF TIMESTAMP (SYSTIMESTAMP - INTERVAL '180' MINUTE);

view EMPLOYEES_MINUS3_HOURS_V created.
```

Oracle Flashback Version Query

Flashback Version Query is used to retrieve metadata and historical data for a specific interval. The interval can be specified by two timestamps or by two SCNs. The metadata returned includes the start and end time a version existed, type of DML operation used to create it, and the identity of the transaction that created each row version. The VERSIONS BETWEEN clause of a SELECT statement is used to generate a Flashback Version Query. The syntax of the VERSIONS BETWEEN clause is: VERSIONS {BETWEEN {SCN | TIMESTAMP} start AND end}.

The Pseudocolumns returned by a Flashback version query are:

- **VERSIONS_START[SCN/TIME]** -- Starting System Change Number (SCN) or TIMESTAMP when the row version was created. NULL if version is from before the start value.
- **VERSIONS_END[SCN/TIME]** -- SCN or TIMESTAMP when the row version expired. If NULL, then either the row version was current at the time of the query or the row is for a DELETE operation.
- **VERSIONS_XID** -- Identifier of the transaction that created the row version.
- **VERSIONS_OPERATION** -- Operation performed by the transaction: I for insertion, D for deletion, or U for update. The version is that of the row that was inserted, deleted, or updated.

A given row version is valid starting at VERSIONS_START* up to, but not including, VERSIONS_END*. That is, it is valid for any time 't' such that VERSIONS_START* <= t < VERSIONS_END*. The following three updates were issued against the EMPLOYEES table, with a pause in-between.

```
UPDATE employees SET salary = 97000
WHERE emp_last='McCoy';
UPDATE employees SET salary = 102000
WHERE emp_last='McCoy';
UPDATE employees SET salary = 105000
WHERE emp_last='McCoy';
COMMIT;
```

Then the following Flashback Versions query was run against employees:

```
SELECT versions_starttime, versions_endtime,
       versions_xid, versions_operation AS OP,
       salary
  FROM employees
  VERSIONS BETWEEN TIMESTAMP
     TO_TIMESTAMP('29-MAR-12 11.46.00PM','DD-MON-YY HH:MI:SSAM')
  AND TO_TIMESTAMP('29-MAR-12 11.52.00PM','DD-MON-YY HH:MI:SSAM')
  WHERE emp_last = 'McCoy';


VERSIONS_STARTTIME    VERSIONS_ENDTIME       VERSIONS_XID      OP SALARY
-------------------   --------------------   ----------------  -- ------
29-MAR-12 11.51.08PM                         09000900A9010000  U  105000
29-MAR-12 11.49.50PM  29-MAR-12 11.51.08PM   04001A003F010000  U  102000
29-MAR-12 11.49.02PM  29-MAR-12 11.49.50PM   03002100A2010000  U   97000
                      29-MAR-12 11.49.02PM                         93500
```

From the results above, you see the three updates against the table, each increasing the salary column value. It's clear when each salary value started and ended (save the initial value for which the start time was outside the window, and the end value which is current (and therefore has no end time). You can use VERSIONS_XID with Oracle Flashback Transaction Query to locate the metadata for any of the three transactions. This will include the SQL required to undo the row change and the user responsible for the change.

Oracle Flashback Transaction Query.

A Flashback Transaction Query is used to retrieve metadata and historical data for a single transaction or for all transactions in a supplied interval. The data is generated from the static data dictionary view FLASHBACK_TRANSACTION_QUERY. The Flashback Transaction Query creates a column UNDO_SQL. The SQL text in this field is the logical opposite of the DML operation performed by the transaction shown. The code from this field can usually reverse original transaction within reason (e.g. a SQL_UNDO INSERT operation would be unlikely to insert a row back at the same ROWID from which it was deleted). As a general rule, Oracle Flashback Transaction Query is used in conjunction with an Oracle Flashback Version Query that provides transaction IDs.

```
SELECT operation, start_scn, commit_scn, logon_user
  FROM flashback_transaction_query
    WHERE xid = HEXTORAW('09000900A9010000');
```

```
OPERATION     START_SCN COMMIT_SCN LOGON_USER
------------- --------- ---------- ------------
UNKNOWN         393394     393463  OCPGURU
BEGIN           393394     393463  OCPGURU
```

The following statement uses Oracle Flashback Version Query as a subquery to associate each row version with the LOGON_USER responsible for the row data change.

```
SELECT xid, logon_user
  FROM flashback_transaction_query
    WHERE xid IN (
      SELECT versions_xid
      FROM employees VERSIONS BETWEEN TIMESTAMP
        TO_TIMESTAMP('29-MAR-12 11.40.00 PM',
                     'DD-MON-YY HH:MI:SS AM') AND
        TO_TIMESTAMP('29-MAR-12 11.56.00 PM',
                     'DD-MON-YY HH:MI:SS AM')
    );
```

Create and use external tables

The external tables feature in Oracle allows you to access data in external files as if it were in a table in the database. To create an external table, you must know the file format and record format of the data source that will be used for the table. External tables are created using the ORGANIZATION EXTERNAL option of the CREATE TABLE statement. When creating an external table, you specify the following attributes:

- **TYPE** -- The two external table types are ORACLE_LOADER, and ORACLE_DATAPUMP. The ORACLE_LOADER access driver is the default. It can not write to the file, only read, and the data must come from a text file. The ORACLE_DATAPUMP access driver can read from and write to external binary dump files.
- **DEFAULT DIRECTORY** -- Specifies the default location of the external files. The location must be specified using an Oracle directory object. The directory object must exist prior to the creation of the EXTERNAL TABLE.
- **ACCESS PARAMETERS** -- Specify the information about the external data source required for the access driver to be able to read it. The two access types have distinct parameter

requirements. The access parameters are also referred to as the opaque_format_spec in the CREATE TABLE...ORGANIZATION EXTERNAL statement.

- **LOCATION** -- Indicates the location of the external data. The file locations are paired directory objects and filenames. If no directory is specified, then the default directory object is used.

The following example shows the use of each of these attributes:

```
CREATE TABLE emp_load
  (emp_number        CHAR(5),
   emp_dob           CHAR(20),
   emp_last_name     CHAR(20),
   emp_first_name    CHAR(15),
   emp_middle_name CHAR(15),
   emp_hire_date     DATE)
ORGANIZATION EXTERNAL
  (TYPE ORACLE_LOADER
   DEFAULT DIRECTORY def_dir1
   ACCESS PARAMETERS
     (RECORDS DELIMITED BY NEWLINE
      FIELDS (emp_number        CHAR(2),
              emp_dob           CHAR(20),
              emp_last_name     CHAR(18),
              emp_first_name    CHAR(11),
              emp_middle_name CHAR(11),
              emp_hire_date     CHAR(10)
                  date_format DATE mask "mm/dd/yyyy"
             )
     )
   LOCATION ('info.dat')
  );
```

Once created, external tables act in most ways like an internal table. There is no special syntax when querying them via a SELECT statement. It's not possible to create indexes on them and every query against them effectively performs a full-table scan, so performance can be an issue with large files. Even when performing a specific query against what would normally be considered a 'primary key' field, Oracle must scan every single row in the file before the query is complete. Because the files making up an external table are not really part of the database, transferring them between databases is easy.

Manipulating Large Data Sets

This test objective revolves around several techniques to facilitate the insertion or update of large amounts of data in Oracle tables. Specifically it deals with using subqueries for insert and update operations, multi-table INSERTS, the MERGE command, and using FLASHBACK operations to track changes to a table over a period of time.

Manipulate data using subqueries

Subqueries can be used to perform several functions in tandem with DML operations. You need to be familiar with how they can assist in altering data in tables.

SELECT Operations

You can use a subquery in the FROM clause of a SELECT statement. This is known as an inline view and creates a data source for the SELECT statement. Inline views allow you to have all the code needed to support a query in a single location. It's debatable whether or not a SELECT is considered a DML operation, but you are likely to see questions on the exam involving subqueries being used as inline views.

```
SELECT emp_job, avg_sal, min_sal || ' - ' ||  max_sal AS
salary_range
FROM   (SELECT emp_job, AVG(salary) AVG_SAL, MIN(salary)
MIN_SAL, MAX(salary) MAX_SAL
       FROM   employees
       GROUP BY emp_job)
ORDER BY max_sal DESC
```

INSERT Operations

Subqueries are invaluable in copying data from one table to another. Using a subquery as the source for an INSERT is very often useful. It's a rapid way to generate new data, transfer data to another location or create an ad-hoc backup of table data before performing a potentially destructive DML operation.

```
INSERT INTO aircraft_types_bkup
SELECT act_id, act_name, act_body_style, act_decks, act_seats
FROM    aircraft_types;
```

UPDATE Operations

You can use subqueries to update one table based on data in a second. It is possible to use a subquery to generate the data to be used in the update operation. This will often be done with a correlated subquery where the value returned is dependent on data in the table being updated.

```
UPDATE employees
SET    emp_supervisor = (SELECT emp_id
                         FROM    employees
                         WHERE   last_name = 'Newberry')
WHERE  emp_supervisor = 9;
```

Alternately, a subquery in an UPDATE operation might be used to determine which rows should be updated. Again, this would normally be a correlated subquery.

```
UPDATE employees
SET    emp_supervisor = 18
WHERE  emp_supervisor = (SELECT emp_id
                         FROM    employees
                         WHERE   last_name = 'Storm');
```

DELETE Operations

You can use a subquery to delete data from one table based on information in a second. Subqueries used in this fashion will always be part of the WHERE clause.

```
DELETE FROM aircraft_types
WHERE  act_id  NOT IN (SELECT act_id
                       FROM    aircraft_fleet);
```

Describe the features of multitable INSERTs

A multitable INSERT statement allows you to conditionally insert rows returned by a subquery into one or more tables. They're often used in Extract-Transform-Load (ETL) processes when populating data warehouses. They can provide a significant performance enhancement over performing multiple individual INSERT operations.

Use the following types of multitable INSERTs (Unconditional, Conditional and Pivot)

The different types of multitable inserts are:

- **Conditional INSERT FIRST** – Each row returned by the subquery is inserted into the first table for which it matches the condition.
- **Unconditional INSERT ALL** – Each row returned by the subquery is inserted into every target table.
- **Conditional INSERT ALL** – Each row returned by the subquery is inserted into every target table for which it matches the condition.
- **Pivot INSERT** – A variant of the Unconditional INSERT ALL that performs a pivot operation on the data during the insert – turning data from multiple columns in the source subquery into multiple rows in the destination table.

The syntax for a multitable INSERT is:
      INSERT [conditional_insert_clause]
      [insert_into_clause value_clause]
      (subquery)

The syntax of the conditional_insert_clause is:
      [ALL] [FIRST]
      [WHEN condition THEN] [insert_into_clause value_clause]
      [ELSE] [insert_into_clause value_clause]

When the ALL keyword is used, the operation will insert a row into every table for which it matches the condition. When the FIRST keyword is used, the operation will insert a row only into the first table for which it matches the condition. If the ALL keyword is used and no conditions are supplied, then every row returned by the subquery will be inserted into every table supplied in the INSERT statement. On a conditional INSERT, if a row does not evaluate to TRUE on any of the conditions and there is no ELSE, then no action is taken for that row. Multitable inserts cannot be performed on views or remote tables.

Conditional INSERT FIRST

The Conditional INSERT FIRST statement steps through the values returned by the subquery. As each row is returned, it is evaluated against the conditions from the top down. As soon as one of the conditions evaluate to TRUE, the row will be inserted into the appropriate table. Oracle will skip any remaining insertion conditions and begin evaluating the next row returned by the subquery. The example below conditionally inserts employees records into tables indicating they've been with the company >20 years, >15 years, >10 years, or >5 years.

```
INSERT FIRST
  WHEN MONTHS_BETWEEN(SYSDATE, start_date) >= 240 THEN
    INTO emps_20
    VALUES (emp_id, emp_first, emp_last)
  WHEN MONTHS_BETWEEN(SYSDATE, start_date) >= 180 THEN
    INTO emps_15
    VALUES (emp_id, emp_first, emp_last)
  WHEN MONTHS_BETWEEN(SYSDATE, start_date) >= 120 THEN
    INTO emps_10
    VALUES (emp_id, emp_first, emp_last)
  WHEN MONTHS_BETWEEN(SYSDATE, start_date) >= 60 THEN
    INTO emps_5
    VALUES (emp_id, emp_first, emp_last)
SELECT emp_id, emp_first, emp_last, start_date
FROM    employees;

SELECT * FROM emps_5;

EMP_ID EMP_FIRST   EMP_LAST
------ ----------- -----------
     6 Janet       Jeckson
    15 Luke        Skytalker
    16 Dell        Aptop
    17 Noh         Kia
```

```
SELECT * FROM emps_10;

EMP_ID EMP_FIRST   EMP_LAST
------ ----------  ----------
     8 Alf         Alien
     9 Norm        Storm
    13 James       Thomas
    14 John        Picard
     7 Fred        Stoneflint

SELECT * FROM emps_15;

EMP_ID EMP_FIRST   EMP_LAST
------ ----------  ----------
     1 Big         Boss
     2 Adam        Smith
     3 Rick        Jameson
     4 Rob         Stoner
     5 Bill        Abong
    10 John        Jones
    11 Top         Gun
    12 Phil        McCoy

SELECT * FROM emps_20;

no rows selected
```

Unconditional INSERT ALL

The following inserts into the EMP_JOBS and EMP_EMAIL tables all rows returned by the subquery. The column values being inserted into the individual tables do not have to match. Every row returned by the subquery results in two table insertions. In the below example, the employee EMAIL and JOB_ID values are broken out into two new tables due to a new and incomprehensible HR requirement.

```
INSERT ALL
    INTO emp_jobs (employee_id, job_id)
    VALUES (employee_id, job_id)
    INTO emp_email (employee_id, email)
    VALUES (employee_id, email)
SELECT employee_id, job_id, email
FROM   hr.employees;

214 rows inserted.
```

```
SELECT * FROM emp_jobs WHERE employee_id < 110;

EMPLOYEE_ID JOB_ID
----------- ----------
        100 AD_PRES
        101 AD_VP
        102 AD_VP
        103 IT_PROG
        104 IT_PROG
        105 IT_PROG
        106 IT_PROG
        107 IT_PROG
        108 FI_MGR
        109 FI_ACCOUNT


SELECT * FROM emp_email WHERE employee_id < 110;

EMPLOYEE_ID EMAIL
----------- ------------------------
        100 SKING
        101 NKOCHHAR
        102 LDEHAAN
        103 AHUNOLD
        104 BERNST
        105 DAUSTIN
        106 VPATABAL
        107 DLORENTZ
        108 NGREENBE
        109 DFAVIET
```

Conditional INSERT ALL

The conditional INSERT ALL simply adds a condition that must be evaluated before the insertion occurs. As each row is returned by the subquery, Oracle checks it against the condition to see if it evaluates to TRUE. If so, it will be inserted. If not, Oracle will move to the next condition or to the next subquery row if no more conditions exist. The following query splits up all of the employees evenly among two teams for a company-wide morale-building game of football.

```
INSERT ALL
  WHEN  MOD(ROWNUM,2) = 1 THEN
    INTO emp_shirts (emp_id, emp_first, emp_last)
    VALUES (emp_id, emp_first, emp_last)
  WHEN  MOD(ROWNUM,2) = 0 THEN
    INTO emp_skins (emp_id, emp_first, emp_last)
    VALUES (emp_id, emp_first, emp_last)
SELECT emp_id, emp_first, emp_last
FROM    employees;

17 rows inserted.


SELECT * FROM emp_shirts;

EMP_ID EMP_FIRST  EMP_LAST
------ ---------- ----------
     1 Big        Boss
     3 Rick       Jameson
     5 Bill       Abong
     8 Alf        Alien
    10 John       Jones
    12 Phil       McCoy
    14 John       Picard
    16 Dell       Aptop
     7 Fred       Stoneflint

SELECT * FROM emp_skins;

EMP_ID EMP_FIRST  EMP_LAST
------ ---------- ----------
     2 Adam       Smith
     4 Rob        Stoner
     6 Janet      Jeckson
     9 Norm       Storm
    11 Top        Gun
    13 James      Thomas
    15 Luke       Skytalker
    17 Noh        Kia
```

Pivot INSERT

A Pivot INSERT is used to convert column data in the source subquery into row data in the destination table. Converting columns to rows is generally known as a pivot operation. In the example below, the subquery is run against the SALES_BY_FY table. This table contains sales data for various fiscal years with the numbers broken into columns by quarter. The Pivot

INSERT operation will use the source data to pull the quarterly sales data out into individual rows to the SALES_BY_QUARTER table.

```
DESC sales_by_fy

Name           Null  Type
-----------    ----  -----------
FISCAL_YEAR          VARCHAR2(5)
Q1_SALES             NUMBER
Q2_SALES             NUMBER
Q3_SALES             NUMBER
Q4_SALES             NUMBER


SELECT * FROM sales_by_fy;

FISCAL_YEAR Q1_SALES Q2_SALES Q3_SALES Q4_SALES
----------- -------- -------- -------- --------
2010          250000   300000   175000   180000
2011          225000   280000   195000   189000
2012          270000   310000   187000   192000


INSERT ALL
  INTO sales_by_quarter VALUES (fiscal_year, 1, q1_sales)
  INTO sales_by_quarter VALUES (fiscal_year, 2, q2_sales)
  INTO sales_by_quarter VALUES (fiscal_year, 3, q3_sales)
  INTO sales_by_quarter VALUES (fiscal_year, 4, q4_sales)
  SELECT fiscal_year, q1_sales, q2_sales, q3_sales, q4_sales
  FROM   sales_by_fy;


SELECT *
FROM sales_by_quarter
ORDER BY fiscal_year, quarter;

FISCAL_YEAR QUARTER SALES
----------- ------- -----
2010              1 250000
2010              2 300000
2010              3 175000
2010              4 180000
2011              1 225000
2011              2 280000
2011              3 195000
2011              4 189000
2012              1 270000
2012              2 310000
2012              3 187000
2012              4 192000
```

Merge rows in a table

MERGE is a DML operation that combines aspects of INSERT, UPDATE and DELETE. A single MERGE statement can perform one, two, or all three activities conditionally. There is nothing that can be performed by the MERGE statement that cannot be performed individually by a combination of INSERT, UODATE and DELETE operations. The power of a MERGE statement is in being able to perform multiple activities in a single pass. For ETL activities in particular, a MERGE might be able to significantly improve performance on operations involving a large amount of data. In order to perform MERGE operations, you must have the neccesary rights. There is no MERGE privilege – so you need, SELECT, UPDATE, and DELETE privileges on the appropriate tables in order to perform MERGE operations. The syntax for the MERGE statement is:

```
MERGE INTO dest_table tab_alias1
  USING (source_expr) tab_alias2
  ON (join_condition)
   WHEN MATCHED THEN
    UPDATE SET
      col1 = val1,
      col2 = val2
    DELETE WHERE (del_cond)
    WHEN NOT MATCHED THEN
      INSERT (col_list)
      VALUES (col_values)
```

- **dest_table** – The table for which rows will be inserted, updated, or delted
- **source_expr** – The source of row data for the MERGE, this can be a table, view, or subquery.
- **join_condition** – The condition which is evaluated for each row.
- **del_cond** – Delete row if this condition is met.
- **WHEN MATCHED** – The operation in this clause will be performed when join_condition evaluates to TRUE.
- **WHEN NOT MATCHED** -- The operation in this clause will be performed when join_condition evaluates to FALSE.

An example of this operation follows. The statement is designed to update a backup table to the employees table to match the original. Where employee ids match between the two tables, the backup EMP_ID record is updated to match all the current values in the primary table.

Where the EMP_ID field no longer exists in the primary table, it is deleted from the backup. Where the employee ID does not exist in the backup, it is inserted directly from the primary.

```
MERGE INTO employees_bkup empb
USING (SELECT * FROM employees) emp
ON (empb.emp_id = emp.emp_id)
WHEN MATCHED THEN
UPDATE SET
  empb.afl_id = emp.afl_id,
  empb.emp_first = emp.emp_first,
  empb.emp_last = emp.emp_last,
  empb.emp_job = emp.emp_job,
  empb.emp_supervisor = emp.emp_supervisor,
  empb.salary = emp.salary,
  empb.start_date = emp.start_date
DELETE WHERE (empb.emp_id NOT IN (SELECT emp_id FROM
employees))
WHEN NOT MATCHED THEN
INSERT VALUES (emp.emp_id, emp.afl_id, emp.emp_first,
emp.emp_last,
     emp.emp_job, emp.emp_supervisor, emp.salary,
emp.start_date);
```

A MERGE statement cannot alter the column that is referenced in the join condition of the ON clause.

Track the changes to data over a period of time

The Flashback queries discussed in an earlier section can be used to track data changes. They are useful if you are trying to determine what DML operations have been made to a table recently, possibly in order to repair data that was altered in error. If you know specifically when a change was made, you can use the Flashback Query to find the data that existed prior to that time. If you are unsure of when the change occurred, you could either use multiple Flashback queries at various points in time, or make use of the Flashback Version Query to locate all changes over a time interval. Once an erroneous transaction has been located, you can use the Flashback Transaction Query to generate the SQL required to reverse the transaction. An example of making changes to data in a table and showing the versions of the changed data follow:

```
SELECT emp_first, emp_last, salary
FROM    employees
WHERE   emp_last = 'Picard';

EMP_FIRST   EMP_LAST    SALARY
----------  ----------  ------
John        Picard       94500


UPDATE employees
SET     salary = 49500
WHERE   emp_last = 'Picard';
1 rows updated.

COMMIT;
commited.


UPDATE employees
SET     salary = 57500
WHERE   emp_last = 'Picard';
1 rows updated.


SELECT emp_first, emp_last, salary
FROM    employees
  VERSIONS BETWEEN SCN MINVALUE AND MAXVALUE
WHERE   emp_last = 'Picard';

EMP_FIRST   EMP_LAST    SALARY
----------  ----------  ------
John        Picard       49500
John        Picard       94500
```

Using SCN MINVALUE and MAXVALUE has the effect of showing all versions of the rows returned by the query that are accessible in UNDO. The versions query shows the original value but only one of the two changes that we made to it. The reason the second UPDATE is not shown in the VERSIONS BETWEEN query is because it was never committed. Until a COMMIT happens, there is no transaction.

Generating Reports by Grouping Related Data

This test objective revolves around Oracle's more advanced grouping operations. The ROLLUP, CUBE, GROUPING, and GROUPING SETS capabilities of Oracle SQL are very powerful, but are not features that are as commonly used by most SQL developers. All of them are logical extensions of the capabilities provided by the GROUP BY clause.

The basic GROUP BY clause separates rows from a table into groups based on supplied criteria. Aggregate data from the grouped rows can then be generated using Oracle's aggregate functions and a single value returned for each group:

```
SELECT  act_name, SUM(act_seats) AS TOTAL_SEATS,
        COUNT(*) AS AIRCRAFT_COUNT
FROM    aircraft_fleet_v
GROUP BY act_name
ORDER BY act_name;
```

Use the ROLLUP operation to produce subtotal values

When the ROLLUP keyword is added to the GROUP BY clause of a query, it generates additional rows in the output to display subtotals of the grouped data. In addition, ROLLUP generates a row at the end of the query that supplies a grand total value. The subtotal and grand total rows are called superaggregate groupings. The number of superaggregate rows generated is dependent on the number of expressions supplied in the ROLLUP clause. Given n expressions, it will always produce n+1 groupings. The syntax for a statement including a ROLLUP is:

```
SELECT  [col1, col2, …], aggregate_function(col3)…
FROM    table
[WHERE  condition]
GROUP BY ROLLUP group_by_expr
[HAVING  having_expr]
[ORDER BY  order_by_expr]
```

Below, is an example querying the AIRCRAFT_FLEET_V view again, this time including the airport name in as an additional grouping column. The ROLLUP keyword generates a subtotal row every time the APT_NAME column changes, plus a grand total at the bottom.

```
SELECT apt_name, act_name, SUM(act_seats) AS TOTAL_SEATS,
       COUNT(*) AS AIRCRAFT_COUNT
FROM   aircraft_fleet_v
GROUP BY ROLLUP(apt_name, act_name)
ORDER BY apt_name, act_name;
```

APT_NAME	ACT_NAME	TOTAL_SEATS	AIRCRAFT_COUNT
Atlanta, GA	Boeing 737	200	1
Atlanta, GA	Boeing 757	240	1
Atlanta, GA		440	2
Dallas/Fort Worth	Boeing 747	416	1
Dallas/Fort Worth	Boeing 767	350	1
Dallas/Fort Worth		766	2
Miami, FL	Boeing 747	832	2
Miami, FL		832	2
Orlando, FL	Boeing 767	700	2
Orlando, FL		700	2
		2738	8

Use the CUBE operation to produce crosstabulation values

Just as the ROLLUP keyword added to the GROUP BY clause of a query produces subtotals, the CUBE keyword will produce cross-tabulation values. ROLLUP will produce only subtotals for the grouped expressions read from left to right plus a grand total (n+1 groupings). When the CUBE keyword is used, all of the columns used in the GROUP BY clause are cross-referenced to produce a superset of groups. Any aggregate functions in the SELECT list are used with the superaggregate rows to produce summary data. A CUBE will generate subtotals for every possible combination of the supplied expressions plus a grand total. This will produce 2^n groupings (an n-dimensional cube).

A CUBE that is grouped by columns A and B will produce four groupings:
- Row totals grouped by column A alone.
- Row totals grouped by column B alone.
- Row totals grouped by columns A & B.
- A grand total.

The syntax for a statement including a CUBE is:

```
SELECT  [col1, col2, …], aggregate_function(col3)…
FROM    table
[WHERE   condition]
GROUP BY CUBE group_by_expr
[HAVING  having_expr]
[ORDER BY  order_by_expr]
```

Below, is an example querying the AIRCRAFT_FLEET_V view once more, this time using the CUBE rather than the ROLLUP keyword. The CUBE keyword generates the same subtotal rows and grand total row of the ROLLUP, plus an additional four subtotal rows based on the ACT_NAME column but not the APT_NAME column. As defined above, you have rows grouped by A alone (APT_NAME) where the ACT_NAME column is shown as NULL. You have rows grouped by B alone (ACT_NAME) where the APT_NAME column is shown as NULL. Finally you have rows grouped by both A & B columns (neither column is NULL).

APT_NAME	ACT_NAME	TOTAL_SEATS	AIRCRAFT_COUNT
Atlanta, GA	Boeing 737	200	1
Atlanta, GA	Boeing 757	240	1
Atlanta, GA		440	2
Dallas/Fort Worth	Boeing 747	416	1
Dallas/Fort Worth	Boeing 767	350	1
Dallas/Fort Worth		766	2
Miami, FL	Boeing 747	832	2
Miami, FL		832	2
Orlando, FL	Boeing 767	700	2
Orlando, FL		700	2
	Boeing 737	**200**	**1**
	Boeing 747	**1248**	**3**
	Boeing 757	**240**	**1**
	Boeing 767	**1050**	**3**
		2738	8

Use the GROUPING function to identify the row values created by ROLLUP or CUBE

The ROLLUP and CUBE extensions of the GROUP BY clause create superaggregate rows where the set of all values is displayed as NULL. The GROUPING function allows you to distinguish superaggregate rows from regular grouped rows. When passed an expression from the GROUP BY clause, the GROUPING function returns a one if the value of that expression is a NULL representing the set of all values. Otherwise it returns a zero.

```
SELECT apt_name, act_name, SUM(act_seats) AS TOTAL_SEATS,
       COUNT(*) AS AIRCRAFT_COUNT,
       GROUPING(ACT_NAME) GRP_APT_NAME
FROM   aircraft_fleet_v
GROUP BY ROLLUP(apt_name, act_name)
ORDER BY apt_name, act_name;
```

APT_NAME	ACT_NAME	TOTAL_SEATS	AC_COUNT	GRP
Atlanta, GA	Boeing 737	200	1	0
Atlanta, GA	Boeing 757	240	1	0
Atlanta, GA		440	2	1
Dallas/Fort Worth	Boeing 747	416	1	0
Dallas/Fort Worth	Boeing 767	350	1	0
Dallas/Fort Worth		766	2	1
Miami, FL	Boeing 747	832	2	0
Miami, FL		832	2	1
Orlando, FL	Boeing 767	700	2	0
Orlando, FL		700	2	1
		2738	8	1

Use GROUPING SETS to produce a single result set

The GROUPING SETS capability is another extension of the GROUP BY clause. It allows you to specify multiple groupings of data and prune any aggregates that you don't require. The database computes all of the groupings listed in the GROUPING SETS clause and combines the results with a UNION ALL operation. The result set can include duplicate rows because the UNION ALL operation will not remove duplicates.

```
SELECT [col1, col2, …], aggregate_function(col3)…
FROM   table
[WHERE  condition]
GROUP BY
GROUPING SETS
  (group_by_expr1),
  (group_by_expr2),
  (…)
[HAVING  having_expr]
[ORDER BY  order_by_expr]
```

The following example finds the number of aircraft aggregated for four specified column groups: (APT_NAME, ACT_NAME), (APT_NAME),

(ACT_BODY_STYLE) and (ACT_DECKS). To get this information without the
GROUPING SETS syntax, you would have to run four separate GROUP BY
queries and UNION ALL them, or run a query with a CUBE of the three
columns and then remove eleven of the sixteen groups thus generated.
When there is a need for generating multiple sets like this, GROUPING
SETS is faster than either option, and its performance benefit gets larger
as the number of sets increases. Only one pass through the data is
required to generate all of the requested sets.

```
SELECT apt_name, act_name, act_body_style AS BSTYLE,
       act_decks, COUNT(*) AS AC_CNT
FROM   aircraft_fleet_v
GROUP BY GROUPING SETS
  (
    (apt_name, act_name),
    (apt_name),
    (act_body_style),
    (act_decks)
  );
```

APT_NAME	ACT_NAME	BSTYLE	ACT_DECKS	AC_CNT
Miami, FL	Boeing 747			2
Miami, FL				2
Atlanta, GA	Boeing 737			1
Atlanta, GA	Boeing 757			1
Atlanta, GA				2
Orlando, FL	Boeing 767			2
Orlando, FL				2
Dallas/Fort Worth	Boeing 747			1
Dallas/Fort Worth	Boeing 767			1
Dallas/Fort Worth				2
		Wide		6
		Narrow		2
			Single	5
			Double	3

Managing Data in Different Time Zones

The DATE data type of Oracle has been around since the dawn of time, or at least since V6 which is the first release I ever worked with. In Release 9i of Oracle, new timestamp data types were introduced that added the ability to track time zone information and fractional seconds. The intent of this test objective is to ensure that you know who to make use of the features provided by these types.

Use Various datetime functions

The complete list of datetime data types in oracle are: DATE, TIMESTAMP, TIMESTAMP WITH TIME ZONE, and TIMESTAMP WITH LOCAL TIME ZONE. There are also two data types that store date interval values rather than the date values themselves. These are INTERVAL YEAR TO MONTH and INTERVAL DAY TO SECOND. The definitions of the various TIMESTAMP data types are:

- **TIMESTAMP** -- This data type is an extension of the DATE data type. It stores the year, month, and day of the DATE data type, plus hour, minute, and second values. Unlike the DATE type, TIMESTAMP can store fractional seconds up to a precision of 9 (the default is 6).
- **TIMESTAMP WITH TIME ZONE** – This is a variant of TIMESTAMP that includes a time zone region name or a time zone offset in its value. The time zone offset is the difference (in hours and minutes) between local time and UTC (Coordinated Universal Time).
- **TIMESTAMP WITH LOCAL TIME ZONE** -- Another variant of TIMESTAMP with time zone information. It differs from TIMESTAMP WITH TIME ZONE in that data is normalized to the database time zone. When a user retrieves the data, Oracle returns it in the user's local session time zone.

The TIMESTAMP data type includes the following fields:

- **YEAR** -- -4712 to 9999 (including year 0)
- **MONTH** – 01 to 12
- **DAY** – 01 to 31
- **HOUR** – 00 to 23
- **MINUTE** – 00 to 59
- **SECOND** – 00 to 59.9(n) WHERE 9(n) is precision
- **TIMEZONE_HOUR** -- -12 to 14
- **TIMEZONE_MINUTE** – 00 to 59

The time zone of the current Oracle session is stored in the session parameter TIME_ZONE. It can be set using the ALTER SESSION command to the database time zone, the operating system time zone, an offset from UTC, or a named time zone region.

```
ALTER SESSION SET TIME_ZONE = dbtimezone;
```

There are several functions available in Oracle for returning the current date and time. In order for them to be meaningful, you must understand the definitions of values they each return.

- **SYSDATE** -- Returns the current date and time of the OS on which the database resides in data type DATE.
- **CURRENT_DATE** -- Returns the current date and time in the session time zone, in data type DATE.
- **CURRENT_TIMESTAMP** -- Returns the current date and time in the session time zone, in data type TIMESTAMP WITH TIME ZONE.
- **LOCALTIMESTAMP** -- Returns the current date and time in the session time zone, in data type TIMESTAMP.

The example below shows the different results obtained from the four functions:

```
ALTER SESSION SET NLS_DATE_FORMAT = 'DD-MON-YY HH:MI:SS AM';
ALTER SESSION SET TIME_ZONE = '-7:00';
```

```
SELECT SYSDATE, CURRENT_DATE,
FROM    dual;

SYSDATE                     CURRENT_DATE
--------------------- ---------------------
27-MAR-12 08:15:41 PM  27-MAR-12 05:15:41 PM


SELECT CURRENT_TIMESTAMP, LOCALTIMESTAMP
FROM    dual;

CURRENT_TIMESTAMP
------------------------------------
27-MAR-12 05.15.41.219000000 PM -07:00

LOCALTIMESTAMP
-------------------------------
27-MAR-12 05.15.41.219000000 PM
```

You can determine the difference (if any) between the session and database time zones by the use of the DBTIMEZONE and SESSIONTIMEZONE functions:

```
SELECT DBTIMEZONE, SESSIONTIMEZONE FROM dual;

DBTIMEZONE SESSIONTIMEZONE
---------- ---------------
+00:00       -07:00
```

Interval data types store the difference between two datetime values. The two interval data types are:

- **INTERVAL YEAR TO MONTH** – Stores an interval that can contain years and months.
- **INTERVAL DAY TO SECOND** – Stores an interval that can contain days, hours, minutes, and seconds (including fractional seconds).

Intervals can only be compared and assignable with other intervals of the same type. It is not possible to compare an INTERVAL YEAR TO MONTH with an INTERVAL DAY TO SECOND.

```
CREATE TABLE ocp_interval_tab (
y_to_m_int INTERVAL YEAR(4) TO MONTH,
d_to_s_int INTERVAL DAY(3) TO SECOND);
```

```
INSERT INTO ocp_interval_tab
VALUES (TO_YMINTERVAL('06-11'),
        TO_DSINTERVAL('05 02:21:19'));
1 rows inserted.

INSERT INTO ocp_interval_tab
VALUES (TO_YMINTERVAL('09-09'),
        TO_DSINTERVAL('22 12:21:34'));
1 rows inserted.

INSERT INTO ocp_interval_tab
VALUES (TO_YMINTERVAL('02-03'),
        TO_DSINTERVAL('45 10:37:43'));
1 rows inserted.

SELECT *
FROM   ocp_interval_tab;

Y_TO_M_INT  D_TO_S_INT
----------- -------------
9-9          22 12:21:34.0
2-3          45 10:37:43.0
6-11         5 2:21:19.0
```

There are numerous functions in Oracle that relate to the timezone-aware and interval data types. For a complete list, you should consult the Oracle SQL Reference Manual. A partial list of the available functions is:

- **EXTRACT** -- Extracts and returns the value of a specified datetime field from a datetime or interval value expression
- **FROM_TZ** -- Converts a TIMESTAMP value at a time zone to a TIMESTAMP WITH TIME ZONE value
- **NUMTOYMINTERVAL** -- Converts number to an INTERVAL YEAR TO MONTH literal
- **SYS_EXTRACT_UTC** -- Extracts the UTC from a datetime with time zone offset
- **TO_DSINTERVAL** -- Converts a character string data type to a value of INTERVAL DAY TO SECOND data type
- **TO_TIMESTAMP** -- Converts a character string data type to a value of TIMESTAMP data type
- **TO_TIMESTAMP_TZ** -- Converts a character string data type to a value of the TIMESTAMP WITH TIME ZONE data type

- **TO_YMINTERVAL** -- Converts a character string data type to a value of the INTERVAL YEAR TO MONTH data type
- **TZ_OFFSET** -- Returns the time zone offset that corresponds to the entered value, based on the date that the statement is executed

Examples of each of the above follow:

EXTRACT

```
SELECT EXTRACT(YEAR FROM SYSDATE) AS ext_year,
       EXTRACT(MONTH FROM SYSDATE) AS ext_month
FROM   dual;

EXT_YEAR EXT_MONTH
-------- ---------
    2012         3
```

FROM_TZ

```
SELECT FROM_TZ(TIMESTAMP'2012-03-25 10:15:00',
               'US/Central') ftz_pst,
       FROM_TZ(TIMESTAMP'2012-03-25 10:15:00',
               'Pacific/Pago_Pago') ftz_pp
FROM   dual;

FTZ_PST
------------------------------------------------
25-MAR-12 10.15.00.000000000 AM US/CENTRAL

FTZ_PP
------------------------------------------------
25-MAR-12 10.15.00.000000000 AM PACIFIC/PAGO_PA
```

NUMTOYMINTERVAL

```
SELECT NUMTOYMINTERVAL(1,'YEAR') YEAR_INTVL,
       NUMTOYMINTERVAL(1,'MONTH') MONTH_INTVL
FROM   dual;

YEAR_INTVL  MONTH_INTVL
----------- -----------
1-0         0-1
```

SYS_EXTRACT_UTC

```
SELECT SYS_EXTRACT_UTC(TIMESTAMP '2012-03-25 11:30:00.00 -
07:00')
FROM    dual;

SYS_EXTRACT_UTC(TIMESTAMP'2012-03-2511:30:00.00-07:00')
-------------------------------------------------------
25-MAR-12 06.30.00.000000000 PM
```

TO_DSINTERVAL

```
SELECT TO_CHAR(SYSDATE, 'DD-MON-YYYY HH:MI:SS AM')
        AS SYSDATE_PRE,
       SYSDATE + TO_DSINTERVAL('15 07:30:20')
        AS SD_PLUS_DSINT
FROM    dual;

SYSDATE_PRE                      SD_PLUS_DSINT
-------------------------------- ----------------------
27-MAR-2012 08:37:51 PM          12-APR-12 04:08:11 AM
```

TO_TIMESTAMP

```
SELECT TO_TIMESTAMP('25-MAR-2012 10:34:00',
                    'DD-MON-YYYY HH24:MI:SS') AS TTS
FROM    dual;

TTS
-----------------------------------------------------------
25-MAR-12 10.34.00.000000000 AM
```

TO_TIMESTAMP_TZ

```
SELECT TO_TIMESTAMP_TZ('25-MAR-2012 10:34:00',
                       'DD-MON-YYYY HH24:MI:SS') AS TTZ
FROM    dual;

TTZ
-------------------------------------------------
25-MAR-12 10.34.00.000000000 AM -07:00
```

TO_YMINTERVAL

```
SELECT SYSDATE,
       SYSDATE + TO_YMINTERVAL('02-03') AS SD_PLUS_YMINT
FROM   dual;

SYSDATE                  SD_PLUS_YMINT
--------------------- ----------------------
27-MAR-12 08:40:17 PM  27-JUN-14 08:40:17 PM
```

TZ_OFFSET

```
SELECT TZ_OFFSET(SESSIONTIMEZONE) AS session_tz,
       TZ_OFFSET(DBTIMEZONE) AS db_tz,
       TZ_OFFSET('US/Central') AS cst_tz,
       TZ_OFFSET('US/Pacific') AS pst_tz,
       TZ_OFFSET('Europe/Moscow) AS msc_tz
FROM   dual;

SESSION_TZ DB_TZ   CST_TZ  PST_TZ  MSC_TZ
---------- ------- ------- ------- -------
-07:00      +00:00  -05:00  -07:00  +04:00
```

Retrieving Data Using Subqueries

This exam objective deals with various ways of writing and using subqueries in Oracle SQL. It will describe multi-column subqueries and scalar subqueries. It will introduce the WITH clause and show various uses of correlated subqueries.

Write a multiple-column subquery

Multi-column subqueries are useful when you need to make a comparison between multiple columns in one table with multiple columns in a second table. When evaluating multiple columns via subqueries, the comparison can be either pairwise or nonpairwise. Effectively pairwise simply means that the column values are linked such that all columns from the main query must match all columns returned by a single row of the subquery.

Pairwise Comparison

```
SELECT  first_name, manager_id, department_id
FROM    hr.employees emp1
WHERE   (manager_id, department_id) IN
            (SELECT manager_id, department_id
             FROM   hr.employees emp2
             WHERE  first_name = 'John')
AND     first_name != 'John'

FIRST_NAME           MANAGER_ID DEPARTMENT_ID
-------------------- ---------- -------------
Renske                      123            50
Stephen                     123            50
Joshua                      123            50
Sarah                       123            50
Britney                     123            50
Samuel                      123            50
Vance                       123            50
Karen                       100            80
Alberto                     100            80
Gerald                      100            80
Eleni                       100            80
Daniel                      108           100
Ismael                      108           100
Jose Manuel                 108           100
Luis                        108           100
```

NonPairwise Comparison

```
SELECT  first_name, manager_id, department_id
FROM    hr.employees emp1
WHERE   manager_id IN
            (SELECT manager_id
             FROM   hr.employees emp2
             WHERE  first_name = 'John')
AND     department_id IN
            (SELECT department_id
             FROM   hr.employees emp2
             WHERE  first_name = 'John')
AND     first_name != 'John'

FIRST_NAME             MANAGER_ID DEPARTMENT_ID
-------------------    ---------- -------------
Matthew                       100            50
Adam                          100            50
Payam                         100            50
Shanta                        100            50
Kevin                         100            50
Renske                        123            50
Stephen                       123            50
Joshua                        123            50
Sarah                         123            50
Britney                       123            50
Samuel                        123            50
Vance                         123            50
Karen                         100            80
Alberto                       100            80
Gerald                        100            80
Eleni                         100            80
Daniel                        108           100
Ismael                        108           100
Jose Manuel                   108           100
Luis                          108           100
```

The non-pairwise comparison returns five extra rows, for manager-department combinations that do not exist for any employee named John. The pairwise comparison ensures that both conditions are met concurrently.

Use scalar subqueries in SQL

A scalar subquery returns exactly one row and one column value. If a scalar subquery returns zero rows, then the value of the scalar subquery expression is NULL. If a scalar subquery returns more than one row, then Oracle returns an error. It's possible to use a scalar subquery expression in almost any place that calls for an expression (expr). A scalar subquery is always enclosed in its own parentheses, even if the location where it is used already positions it within parentheses (e.g. if it is used as the argument to a function).

Scalar subqueries are valid in all clauses of a SELECT except for GROUP BY. They are valid in the SET and WHERE clauses of an UPDATE. They are valid in the WHERE clause of a DELETE.

Beyond that, scalar subqueries are not valid in the following places:
- As default values for columns
- In the RETURNING clause of DML statements
- As the basis of a function-based index
- In CHECK constraints

```
SELECT apt_name, apt_abbr,
       (SELECT COUNT(*)
        FROM   aircraft_fleet afl
        WHERE  afl.apt_id = apt.apt_id) AS AC_COUNT
FROM   airports apt
ORDER BY apt_name;

APT_NAME                   APT_ABBR AC_COUNT
-------------------------- -------- --------
Atlanta, GA                ATL             2
Dallas/Fort Worth          DFW             2
Jacksonville, FL           JAX             0
Miami, FL                  MIA             2
Orlando, FL                MCO             2
```

Solve problems with correlated subqueries

A correlated query occurs when a nested subquery references a column value from table in a parent query one or more levels above the subquery. A correlated subquery is executed once for each row processed by the referenced parent statement. When columns in the subquery comparison have not been qualified, Oracle resolves them by looking first at the subquery and then in the tables in the parent statement. If a column name that exists in both tables is used inside the subquery and is not qualified, Oracle will treat it as belonging to the subquery table. Best practice is to qualify all such column comparisons with the proper table or alias to avoid unintended behavior. Correlated subqueries provide solutions for questions for which the answer depends on a value in each row returned by the parent statement.

```
SELECT  emp_first, emp_last, emp_job, salary
FROM    employees emp1
WHERE   salary < (SELECT AVG(salary)
                  FROM    employees emp2
                  WHERE   emp1.emp_job = emp2.emp_job);
```

EMP_FIRST	EMP_LAST	EMP_JOB	SALARY
Rick	Jameson	SVP	145200
Bill	Abong	VP	123500
Alf	Alien	SrDir	110500
John	Picard	Pilot	49500
Dell	Aptop	Pilot	87500

Update and delete rows using correlated subqueries

Following are examples of using correlated subqueries to DELETE from and UPDATE data based on correlated subqueries. The first example deletes any rows from the AIRCRAFT_TYPES table that do not currently exist in the AIRCRAFT_FLEET table.

```
DELETE
FROM    aircraft_types act
WHERE   0 = (SELECT COUNT(*)
             FROM    aircraft_fleet afl
             WHERE   afl.act_id = act.act_id);
```

The following example gives a 5% raise to all of the pilots currently below the average pilot salary .

```
UPDATE  employees
SET     salary = TRUNC(salary * 1.05)
WHERE   salary < (SELECT AVG(salary)
                  FROM    employees emp2
                  WHERE   emp1.emp_job = emp2.emp_job)
AND     emp_job = 'Pilot';
```

Use the EXISTS and NOT EXISTS operators

The EXISTS operator is used to test for the existence of any rows returned by a subquery. When Oracle is testing the condition for an exists operator, the subquery will be executed. If any result row is returned by the subquery, the condition is flagged as TRUE and the execution of the subquery stops. For this reason, EXISTS can be faster than other operations that evaluate the same way. For example, you could have a subquery that performs a SELECT COUNT(*) and the outer query looks for a value greater than zero. This would have the same effect as an EXISTS against the subquery using SELECT * with the same conditions. However, the COUNT(*) operation would have to process every matching row of the subquery before returning a result whereas an EXISTS that evaluates to TRUE would stop after hitting a single row.

```
SELECT department_id, department_name
FROM    hr.departments dpt
WHERE   EXISTS (SELECT department_id
               FROM    hr.employees emp
               WHERE   dpt.department_id = emp.department_id)

DEPARTMENT_ID DEPARTMENT_NAME
------------- ----------------------------
           10 Administration
           20 Marketing
           30 Purchasing
           40 Human Resources
           50 Shipping
           60 IT
           70 Public Relations
           80 Sales
           90 Executive
          100 Finance
          110 Accounting
```

The NOT EXISTS operator performs the exact opposite evaluation. If any row is returned by the subquery, a FALSE value is returned and the subquery stops processing further rows.

```
SELECT department_id, department_name
FROM    hr.departments dpt
WHERE   NOT EXISTS (SELECT department_id
                    FROM    hr.employees emp
                    WHERE   dpt.department_id =
emp.department_id)

DEPARTMENT_ID DEPARTMENT_NAME
------------- ------------------------------
          120 Treasury
          130 Corporate Tax
          140 Control And Credit
          150 Shareholder Services
          160 Benefits
          170 Manufacturing
          180 Construction
          190 Contracting
          200 Operations
          210 IT Support
          220 NOC
          230 IT Helpdesk
          240 Government Sales
          250 Retail Sales
          260 Recruiting
          270 Payroll
```

Use the WITH clause

The WITH query_name clause allows you to name a subquery block. Once named, the block can be referenced multiple times in the same query. The database treats the query name as either an inline view or as a temporary table. When treated as a temporary table, the results of running the subquery once are stored in the temporary tablespace and used every time the block is called in the query.

You can specify this clause in any top-level SELECT statement and in most types of subqueries. The query name is visible to the main query and to all subsequent subqueries. For recursive subquery factoring, the query name is even visible to the subquery that defines the query name itself.

In the following example the salaries for each department are calculated in the query named DEPT_COSTS. The results of that query are then averaged in the query named AVG_COST and the result used in the SELECT operation to return only the departments for which the costs are above the average.

```
WITH
  dept_costs AS (
    SELECT department_name, SUM(salary) dept_total
    FROM    hr.employees e
            INNER JOIN hr.departments d
            ON e.department_id = d.department_id
    GROUP BY department_name),
  avg_cost AS (
    SELECT SUM(dept_total)/COUNT(*) avg
    FROM    dept_costs)
SELECT *
FROM    dept_costs
WHERE   dept_total > (SELECT avg FROM avg_cost)
ORDER BY department_name;

DEPARTMENT_NAME                       DEPT_TOTAL
----------------------------------    ----------
Sales                                     304500
Shipping                                  156400
```

Hierarchical Retrieval

Some tables contain data that relates rows to each other in such fashion that they can be chained together in a hierarchy (i.e. some rows are 'higher' than other rows). It's possible to select rows from such a table in a hierarchical order using the hierarchical query clause. The classic example of a table with hierarchical data is an employee table where each employee row contains that employee's manager.

Interpret the concept of a hierarchical query

A hierarchical query allows you to make use of existing table data to retrieve rows in a hierarchical format. The data is not stored in the database in a hierarchical fashion, and the query doesn't generate a hierarchy – it just uses a method known as tree walking to retrieve the rows in a way that allows the hierarchy to be built and displayed. Tables with data that relates in this fashion can also be said to have a tree structure. Rows in the table will relate to a parent record or a child record, or both. Oracle's hierarchical query capability allows you to specify a starting point and a direction such that you determine which rows act as the parent and which the child.

The syntax for a hierarchical query is:

```
SELECT [LEVEL], column, expr...
FROM TABLE
[WHERE condition]
[START WITH condition]
[CONNECT BY PRIOR condition];
```

- **LEVEL** – Displays the level of the hierarchy. The top level would be one. Children of that level two, Grandchildren three, and so forth.
- **START WITH** -- Defines the root row(s) of the hierarchy.
- **CONNECT BY PRIOR** -- Defines the relationship between parent rows and child rows of the hierarchy.

When walking through the tree structure in a hierarchical query, Oracle will begin with the row identified in the START WITH clause and utilize the data from the CONNECT BY clause to follow through each link in the chain. To be a true hierarchical query, the CONNECT BY and START WITH clauses are required.

Create a tree-structured report

The root record of the tree is determined by the START WITH condition. This can be a static condition, or the result of a subquery or anything that returns a viable row to act as the root. If the START WITH clause is omitted, the walk is performed with all the rows in the table treated as root rows.

The CONNECT BY PRIOR clause defines the direction that the tree will be walked. To walk down from the top of the tree to the bottom, the PRIOR operator points to the parent row. To walk from the bottom up, the PRIOR operator should point to the child row. If the CONNECT BY has compound conditions, only one condition requires the PRIOR operator, although it is possible to have multiple PRIOR conditions. All of the below are valid conditions:

- CONNECT BY PRIOR emp_id = mgr_id
- CONNECT BY last_name != 'Davidson' AND PRIOR emp_id = mgr_id
- CONNECT BY PRIOR emp_id = mgr_id and PRIOR cust_rep_id = cust_id

PRIOR is most commonly used when comparing column values with the equality operator and can be on either side of the operator. Operators other than the equal sign can be used, however, using them can result in an infinite loop through the possible combinations. Oracle detects such loop at run time and returns an error.

```
SELECT level, emp_first, emp_last, emp_job
FROM    employees emp
START WITH emp_supervisor IS NULL
CONNECT BY PRIOR emp_id = emp_supervisor;

LEVEL EMP_FIRST   EMP_LAST   EMP_JOB
----- ----------  ---------- ----------
    1 Big         Boss       CEO
    2 Adam        Smith      CFO
    2 Rick        Jameson    SVP
    3 Bill        Abong      VP
    4 Fred        Stoneflint SrDir
    2 Rob         Stoner     SVP
    3 Janet       Jeckson    VP
    4 Alf         Alien      SrDir
    5 Norm        Storm      Mgr
    6 John        Jones      Pilot
    6 Top         Gun        Pilot
    6 Phil        McCoy      Pilot
    6 James       Thomas     Pilot
    6 John        Picard     Pilot
    6 Luke        Skytalker  Pilot
    6 Dell        Aptop      Pilot
    6 Noh         Kia        Pilot
```

To build this tree in the opposite direction, the query would select a different START WITH point and reverse the CONNECT BY PRIOR order.

```
SELECT level, emp_first, emp_last, emp_job
FROM    employees emp
START WITH emp_last = 'Kia'
CONNECT BY PRIOR emp_supervisor = emp_id;

LEVEL EMP_FIRST   EMP_LAST   EMP_JOB
----- ----------  ---------- ----------
    1 Noh         Kia        Pilot
    2 Norm        Storm      Mgr
    3 Alf         Alien      SrDir
    4 Janet       Jeckson    VP
    5 Rob         Stoner     SVP
    6 Big         Boss       CEO
```

CONNECT_BY_ROOT is a unary operator that is valid only in hierarchical queries. When you qualify a column with this operator, Oracle returns the column value using data from the root row. The following example shows the hierarchy path all the way to the root record using the CONNECT_BY_ROOT operator and the SYS_CONNECT_BY_PATH function.

```
SELECT emp_last, CONNECT_BY_ROOT emp_last MANAGER,
       SYS_CONNECT_BY_PATH(emp_last, '/') PATH_TO_ROOT
FROM   employees
WHERE  level > 1
CONNECT BY PRIOR emp_id = emp_supervisor
```

```
EMP_LAST    MANAGER     PATH_TO_ROOT
----------  ----------  -----------------------------------------
Jeckson     Stoner      /Stoner/Jeckson
Alien       Stoner      /Stoner/Jeckson/Alien
Storm       Stoner      /Stoner/Jeckson/Alien/Storm
Jones       Stoner      /Stoner/Jeckson/Alien/Storm/Jones
Kia         Stoner      /Stoner/Jeckson/Alien/Storm/Kia
Aptop       Stoner      /Stoner/Jeckson/Alien/Storm/Aptop
Skytalker   Stoner      /Stoner/Jeckson/Alien/Storm/Skytalker
Picard      Stoner      /Stoner/Jeckson/Alien/Storm/Picard
Thomas      Stoner      /Stoner/Jeckson/Alien/Storm/Thomas
McCoy       Stoner      /Stoner/Jeckson/Alien/Storm/McCoy
Gun         Stoner      /Stoner/Jeckson/Alien/Storm/Gun
```

Format hierarchical data

If there is a need to format the order of the rows being returned in a hierarchical query, you should never specify either ORDER BY or GROUP BY, as they will destroy the hierarchical order of the CONNECT BY results. To order rows of siblings of the same parent, you can use the ORDER SIBLINGS BY clause. The following example demonstrates an ORDER BY clause using the SIBLINGS keyword to preserve the hierarchical ordering:

```
SELECT level, emp_first, emp_last, emp_job
FROM   employees emp
START WITH emp_supervisor IS NULL
CONNECT BY PRIOR emp_id = emp_supervisor
ORDER SIBLINGS BY emp_last;
```

```
LEVEL EMP_FIRST   EMP_LAST    EMP_JOB
----- ----------  ----------  ----------
    1 Big         Boss        CEO
    2 Rick        Jameson     SVP
    3 Bill        Abong       VP
    4 Fred        Stoneflint  SrDir
    2 Adam        Smith       CFO
    2 Rob         Stoner      SVP
    3 Janet       Jeckson     VP
    4 Alf         Alien       SrDir
    5 Norm        Storm       Mgr
    6 Dell        Aptop       Pilot
    6 Top         Gun         Pilot
```

```
6 John       Jones       Pilot
6 Noh        Kia         Pilot
6 Phil       McCoy       Pilot
6 John       Picard      Pilot
6 Luke       Skytalker   Pilot
6 James      Thomas      Pilot
```

The LPAD function can be used in conjunction with the LEVEL pseudocolumn to provide formatting to a hierarchical query. The LEVEL column is one for the root records, two for children, three for grandchildren and so forth. Using the LEVEL value as part of the LPAD expression allows you to indent rows based on how many levels they are from the root.

```
SELECT LPAD(emp_first || ' ' || emp_last,
        LENGTH(emp_first || ' ' || emp_last) + (LEVEL-1) *
3, '.') OC_TREE
FROM    employees emp
START WITH emp_supervisor IS NULL
CONNECT BY PRIOR emp_id = emp_supervisor
ORDER SIBLINGS BY emp_last;


OC_TREE
------------------------------
Big Boss
...Rick Jameson
......Bill Abong
.........Fred Stoneflint
...Adam Smith
...Rob Stoner
......Janet Jeckson
.........Alf Alien
............Norm Storm
...............Dell Aptop
...............Top Gun
...............John Jones
...............Noh Kia
...............Phil McCoy
...............John Picard
...............Luke Skytalker
...............James Thomas
```

Exclude branches from the tree structure

It's possible to filter the results of a CONNECT BY query in two locations: the WHERE clause and the CONNECT BY clause. Placing a condition in the WHERE clause filters nodes from the result set. In the context of an org chart, the filter identifies employees not to be returned. By contrast, a condition in the CONNECT BY clause filters branches. Given an org chart example, this filter will eliminate anyone who connects to employees identified by the filter.

Eliminate a Node

In the below example, a condition to the WHERE clause filters out Norm Storm. In the result set, his record is gone, but the employees that report to him remain.

```
SELECT level, emp_first, emp_last, emp_job
FROM    employees emp
WHERE   emp_last != 'Storm'
START WITH emp_supervisor IS NULL
CONNECT BY PRIOR emp_id = emp_supervisor;

LEVEL EMP_FIRST  EMP_LAST    EMP_JOB
----- ---------- ----------  ----------
    1 Big        Boss        CEO
    2 Adam       Smith       CFO
    2 Rick       Jameson     SVP
    3 Bill       Abong       VP
    4 Fred       Stoneflint  SrDir
    2 Rob        Stoner      SVP
    3 Janet      Jeckson     VP
    4 Alf        Alien       SrDir
    6 John       Jones       Pilot
    6 Top        Gun         Pilot
    6 Phil       McCoy       Pilot
    6 James      Thomas      Pilot
    6 John       Picard      Pilot
    6 Luke       Skytalker   Pilot
    6 Dell       Aptop       Pilot
    6 Noh        Kia         Pilot
```

Eliminate a Branch

By contrast, in the below example the condition has been moved to the CONNECT BY clause. In the result set, his record is gone, and so are all the employees that report to him.

```
SELECT level, emp_first, emp_last, emp_job
FROM    employees emp
START WITH emp_supervisor IS NULL
CONNECT BY PRIOR emp_id = emp_supervisor AND emp_last !=
'Storm';
```

LEVEL	EMP_FIRST	EMP_LAST	EMP_JOB
1	Big	Boss	CEO
2	Adam	Smith	CFO
2	Rick	Jameson	SVP
3	Bill	Abong	VP
4	Fred	Stoneflint	SrDir
2	Rob	Stoner	SVP
3	Janet	Jeckson	VP
4	Alf	Alien	SrDir

Regular Expression Support

Regular expressions provide a very powerful and flexible method for describing patterns of text and numbers. The patterns can be used for searching and manipulating data within the Oracle database. Before regular expressions were added to Oracle, adding capabilities comparable to what they provide involved developing complex text parsers.

Using Meta Characters

The regular expression metacharacters are used to identify a specific aspect of the string being processed such as a wildcard, or repeating character; or to provide control over the behavior of the REGEX parsing, such as grouping a pattern or identifying alternates. There are a considerable number of metacharacters available. You won't be expected to code (or identify) extremely complex expressions on the exam. You do need to be familiar with what metacharacters are and how they're used in REGEX functions. You'll also have to recognize some of the more common metacharacters and identify the results of relatively simple regular expressions.

Some common metacharacters are:

- * -- Matches zero or more occurrences
- + -- Matches one or more occurrences
- ? -- Matches zero or one occurrence
- | -- Alternation operator for specifying alternative matches
- ^ -- Matches the beginning of a string by default. In multiline mode, it matches the beginning of any line anywhere within the source string.
- \$ -- Matches the end of a string by default. In multiline mode, it matches the end of any line anywhere within the source string.
- . -- Matches any character in the supported character set except NULL
- ( ) -- Grouping expression, treated as a single subexpression
- {m} -- Matches exactly m times
- {m,} -- Matches at least m times
- {m,n}-- Matches at least m times but no more than n times

- [==] -- Specifies equivalence classes. For example, [=a=] matches all characters having base letter 'a'.
- a-z -- any lowercase letter
- A-Z -- any uppercase letter
- [:alnum:] -- Alphanumeric characters
- [:alpha:] -- Alphabetic characters
- [:ascii:] -- ASCII characters
- [:blank:] -- Space and tab
- [:cntrl:] -- Control characters
- [:digit:] -- Digits (0-9)

Regular Expression Functions

There are numerous regular expression functions available in Oracle. For a complete list, check out the Oracle SQL Reference Guide. Some of the more commonly used ones are:

- **REGEXP_COUNT** -- Returns the number of times a pattern occurs in a source string. It returns an integer indicating the number of occurrences of pattern, or zero if no match is found.

- **REGEXP_INSTR** – Works very much like the standard INSTR function. However, it allows you to search for a string for a regular expression pattern. It returns an integer indicating the beginning or the ending position of the matched substring, depending on the value of the return_option argument. When no match is found, it returns 0.

- **REGEXP_REPLACE** -- Duplicates the functionality of the standard REPLACE function, but allows you to search a string using a regular expression pattern. By default, the function returns source_char with every occurrence of the regular expression pattern replaced with replace_string.

- **REGEXP_SUBSTR** -- Duplicates the functionality of the standard SUBSTR function, but allows you to search a string using a regular expression pattern.

- **REGEXP_LIKE** -- Similar to the standard LIKE condition, except REGEXP_LIKE performs regular expression matching instead of simple pattern matching.

Replacing Patterns

The REGEXP_REPLACE function allows you to directly replace values in a column precisely with the use of regular expressions. The following example takes the phone numbers in the HR.EMPLOYEES tables and replaces the '.' separators with more complex programming. You won't see a REGEXP operation this complex on the test. It's more concerned with you knowing how the functions work than in determining whether you can develop complex expressions without a reference in hand. Oracle is well aware that if you need to develop a complex regular expression in real life, you'll do what I did for this one. Google is a great copilot.

```
SELECT phone_number,
       REGEXP_REPLACE(phone_number,
   '([[:digit:]]{3})\.([[:digit:]]{3})\.([[:digit:]]{4})',
        '(\1)\2-\3') PHONE_NUM_FMTD
FROM   hr.employees
WHERE  job_id = 'IT_PROG'
```

```
PHONE_NUMBER            PHONE_NUM_FMTD
--------------------    --------------
590.423.4567            (590)423-4567
590.423.4568            (590)423-4568
590.423.4569            (590)423-4569
590.423.4560            (590)423-4560
590.423.5567            (590)423-5567
```

The REGEXP_LIKE allows you to locate records with more precise conditions than are possible using a simple LIKE condition. The following looks for employees whose last name starts with 'H' and has either an 'I' or a 'u' as the second letter.

```
SELECT last_name, first_name
FROM   hr.employees
WHERE  REGEXP_LIKE(last_name, '^H[iu]');
```

```
LAST_NAME                       FIRST_NAME
----------------------------    --------------------
Higgins                         Shelley
Himuro                          Guy
Hunold                          Alexander
Hutton                          Alyssa
```

The REGEXP_INSTR function could also be used to locate records. The following looks for last names with a lower-case 'y' in them. I'll grant that you could just as easily do this one with a LIKE operator. There are only so many matching conditions you can do against a really simple data set.

```
SELECT last_name
FROM   hr.employees
WHERE  REGEXP_INSTR(last_name, '[y]') > 0;
```

```
LAST_NAME
------------------------
Dilly
Fay
Feeney
Landry
Nayer
Raphaely
Sully
Taylor
Taylor
Vishney
Zlotkey
```

Regular Expressions and Check Constraints

Regular expressions can be used to make particularly intelligent check constraints. They provide the ability to cram a significant amount of logic into a single function. The following example shows the creation of a check constraint that verifies only valid email addresses are entered into the employee table.

```
ALTER TABLE employees
   ADD CONSTRAINT email_ck
   CHECK(REGEXP_LIKE(email,
       '[a-zA-Z0-9._%-]+@[a-zA-Z0-9._%-]+\.[a-zA-Z]{2,4}'))
   NOVALIDATE;
```

ABOUT THE AUTHOR

Matthew Morris has worked with the Oracle database since 1996 when he worked in the RDBMS support team for Oracle Support Services. Employed by Oracle for over eleven years in support and development positions, Matthew was an early adopter of the Oracle Certified Professional program. He was one of the first one hundred Oracle Certified Database Administrators (version 7.3) and was also in the first hundred to become an Oracle Certified Forms Developer. In the years since, he has upgraded his Database Administrator certification for releases 8i, 9i, 10G and 11G, and added the Application Express Expert and the Oracle SQL Expert certifications. Outside of Oracle, he has CompTIA certifications in Linux+ and Security+.

Matthew is an experienced Database Administrator and PL/SQL developer and has been creating Web applications with Oracle Application Express since the early days of its release. He is currently employed as a Database Engineer with Computer Sciences Corporation developing enterprise applications.

Made in the USA
San Bernardino, CA
07 March 2013